ADVANCED-LEVEL MENUS
GRADES 3–5

W9-BAF-769

Differentiating Instruction With Menus

Math

ADVANCED-LEVEL MENUS
GRADES 3–5

Differentiating Instruction With Menus

Math

Laurie E. Westphal

Prufrock Press Inc.
Waco, Texas

Library of Congress Cataloging-in-Publication Data

Westphal, Laurie E., 1967–
  Differentiating instruction with menus. Math / Laurie E. Westphal.
    p. cm.
  ISBN-13: 978-1-59363-226-7 (pbk.)
  ISBN-10: 1-59363-226-6 (pbk.)
  1. Unit method of teaching. 2. Mathematics—Study and teaching. 3. Critical thinking. 4. Cognitive learning. I. Title. II. Title: Math.
  QA20.U55W47 2007
    510.71—dc22
                            2007000372

Copyright ©2007 Prufrock Press Inc.

Edited by Jennifer Robins
Production Design by Marjorie Parker

ISBN-13: 978-1-59363-226-7

The purchase of this book entitles the buyer to reproduce student activity pages for single classroom use only. Other use requires written permission of publisher. All rights reserved.

At the time of this book's publication, all facts and figures cited are the most current available; all telephone numbers, addresses, and website URLs are accurate and active; all publications, organizations, websites, and other resources exist as described in this book; and all have been verified. The author and Prufrock Press make no warranty or guarantee concerning the information and materials given out by organizations or content found at websites, and we are not responsible for any changes that occur after this book's publication. If you find an error or believe that a resource listed here is not as described, please contact Prufrock Press.

Prufrock Press Inc.
P.O. Box 8813
Waco, TX 76714-8813
Phone: (800) 998-2208
Fax: (800) 240-0333
http://www.prufrock.com

CONTENTS

THE MENUS   35

CHAPTER 1

Choice

"**O**h my gosh! THAAAAANK YOU!" exclaimed one of my students as he fell to his knees dramatically in the middle of my classroom. I had just handed out a List menu on the periodic table and told my students they would be able to choose how they wanted to learn the material.

Why Is Choice Important?

Ask adults whether they would prefer to choose what to do or be told what to do, and of course, they are going to say they would prefer to have a choice. Students have the same feelings. Although they may not stand up and demand a choice if none are present, they benefit in many ways from having them.

One benefit of choice is its ability to meet the needs of so many different students and their learning styles. The Dunedin College of Education (Keen, 2001) conducted a research study on the preferred learning styles of 250 gifted students. Students were asked to rank different learning options. Of the 13 different options described to the students, only one option did not receive at least one negative response, and that was the option of having choice. Although all students have different learning styles and preferences, choice is the one option that meets all students' needs. Students are going to choose what best fits their learning styles and educational needs.

> ## "I am different in the way I do stuff. I like to build stuff with my hands."
> *—Sixth-grade student, when asked why he enjoyed activities that allow choice*

Another benefit of choice is a greater sense of independence for the students. What a powerful feeling! Students will be designing and creating a product based on what they envision, rather than what their teacher envisions. When students would enter my middle-school classroom, they often had been trained by previous teachers to produce exactly what the teacher wanted, not what the students thought would be best. Teaching my students that what they envision could be correct (and wonderful) was often a struggle. "Is this what you want?" or "Is this right?" were popular questions as we started the school year. Allowing students to have choices in the products they create to show their learning helps create independence at an early age.

Strengthened student focus on the required content is a third benefit. When students have choices in the activities they wish to complete, they are more focused on the learning that leads to their choice product. Students become excited when they learn information that can help them develop a product they would like to create. Students pay close attention to instruction and have an immediate application for the knowledge being presented in class. Also, if students are focused, they are less likely to be off task during instruction.

Many a great educator has referred to the idea that the best learning takes place when the students have a desire to learn. Some students have a desire to learn anything that is new to them; others do not want to learn anything unless it is of interest to them. By incorporating different activities from which to choose, students stretch beyond what they already know, and teachers create a void that needs to be filled. This void leads to a desire to learn.

How Can Teachers Provide Choices?

> "The GT students seem to get more involved in assignments when they have choice. They have so many creative ideas and the menus give them the opportunity to use them."
>
> —*Social studies teacher, when asked how students respond to having choices*

When people go to a restaurant, the common goal is to find something on the menu to satisfy their hunger. Students come into our classrooms having a hunger, as well—a hunger for learning. Choice menus are a way of allowing our students to choose how they would like to satisfy that hunger. At the very least, a menu is a list of choices that students use to choose an activity (or activities) they would like to complete to show what they have learned. At best, it is a complex system in which students earn points by making choices from different areas of study. All menus should also incorporate a free-choice option for those "picky eaters" who would like to make a special order to satisfy their learning hunger.

The next few sections provide examples of the main types of menus that will be used in this book. Each menu has its own benefits, limitations or drawbacks, and time considerations. An explanation of the free-choice option and its management will follow the information on each type of menu.

Tic-Tac-Toe Menu

> "Sometimes I only liked two, but I had to do three."
>
> —*Second-grade student, when asked what he liked least about a menu used in his classroom*

Description

The Tic-Tac-Toe menu (see Figure 1.1) is a basic menu that contains a total of eight predetermined choices and one free choice for students. All choices are created at the same level of Bloom's Revised taxonomy (Anderson & Krathwohl, 2001). Each choice carries the same weight for grading and has similar expectations for completion time and effort.

Benefits

Flexibility. This menu can cover one topic in depth, or three different objectives. When this menu covers just one objective, students have the option of completing three projects in a tic-tac-toe pattern, or simply picking three from the menu. When it covers three objectives, students will need to complete a tic-tac-toe pattern (one in each column or row) to be sure they have completed one activity from each objective.

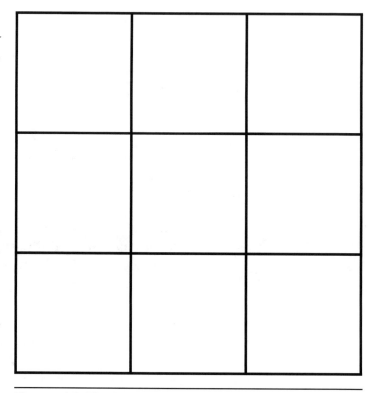

Figure 1.1. Tic-tac-toe menu.

Friendly Design. Students quickly understand how to use this menu.

Weighting. All projects are equally weighted, so recording grades and maintaining paperwork is easily accomplished with this menu.

Limitations

Few Topics. These menus only cover one or three topics.

Short Time Period. They are intended for shorter periods of time, between 1–3 weeks.

Student Compromise. Although this menu does allow choice, a student will sometimes have to compromise and complete an activity he or she would not have chosen because it completes the required tic-tac-toe. (This is not always bad, though!)

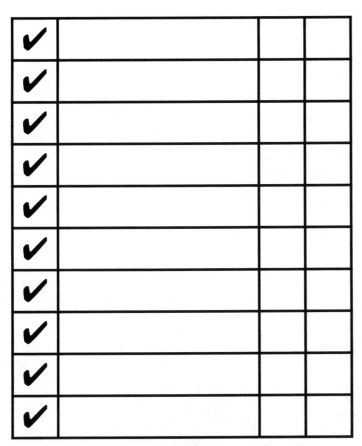

Figure 1.2. List menu.

Time Considerations

These menus are usually intended for shorter amounts of completion time—at the most, they should take 3 weeks. If it focuses on one topic in depth, the menu can be completed in one week.

List Menu

Description

The List menu (see Figure 1.2), or Challenge List, is a more complex menu than the Tic-Tac-Toe menu, with a total of at least 10 predetermined choices, each with its own point value, and at least one free choice for students. Choices are simply listed with assigned points based on the levels of Bloom's Revised taxonomy. The choices carry different weights and have different expectations for completion time and effort. A point criterion is set forth that equals 100%, and students choose how they wish to attain that point goal.

Benefits

Responsibility. Students have complete control over their grades. They really like the idea that they can guarantee their grade if they complete the required work. If they lose points on one of the chosen assignments, they can complete another to be sure they have met their goal points.

Concept Reinforcement. This menu also allows for an in-depth study of material; however, with the different levels of Bloom's Revised taxonomy being represented, students who are still learning the concepts can choose some of the lower level point value projects to reinforce the basics before jumping into the higher level activities.

Limitations

Few Topics. This menu is best used for one topic in depth, although it can be used for up to three different topics, as well.

Cannot Guarantee Objectives. If it is used for three topics, it is possible for a student to not have to complete an activity for each objective, depending on the choices he or she makes.

Preparation. Teachers need to have all materials ready at the beginning of the unit for students to be able to choose any of the activities on the list, which requires advance planning.

Time Considerations

The List menus are usually intended for shorter amounts of completion time—at the most, 2 weeks.

2-5-8 Menu

"My favorite menu is the 2-5-8 kind. It's easy to understand and I can pick just what I want to do."

—Fourth-grade student, when asked about his favorite type of menu

Description

A 2-5-8 menu (see Figure 1.3; Magner, 2000) is a variation of the List Menu, with a total of at least eight predetermined choices: at least two choices with a point value of two, at least four choices with a point value of five, and at least two choices with a point value of eight. Choices are assigned points based on the levels of Bloom's Revised taxonomy. Choices with a point value of two represent the *remember* and *understand* levels, choices with a point value of five represent the *apply* and *analyze* levels, and choices with a point value of eight represent the *evaluate* and *create* levels. All levels of choices carry different weights and have different expectations for completion time and effort.

Figure 1.3. 2-5-8 menu.

Students are expected to earn 10 points for a 100%. Students choose what combination they would like to use to attain that point goal.

Benefits

Responsibility. With this menu, students still have complete control over their grades.

Guaranteed Activity. This menu's design is also set up in such a way that students must complete at least one activity at a higher level of Bloom's Revised taxonomy in order to reach their point goal.

Limitations

One Topic. Although it can be used for more than one topic, this menu works best with in-depth study of one topic.

No Free Choice. By nature, it does not allow students to propose their own free choice, because point values need to be assigned based on Bloom's Revised taxonomy.

Higher Level Thinking. Students will complete only one activity at a higher level of thinking.

Time Considerations

The 2-5-8 menus are usually intended for a shorter amount of completion time—at the most, one week.

Baseball Menu

Description

This menu (see Figure 1.4) is a baseball-based variation on the List menu with a total of at least 20 predetermined choices: choices are given values as singles, doubles, triples, or home runs based on the levels of Bloom's Revised taxonomy. Singles represent the *remember* and *understand* levels; doubles, the *apply* and *analyze* levels; triples, the *evaluate* level; and home runs, the *create* level. All levels of choices carry different weights and have different expectations for completion time and effort. Students are expected to earn a certain number of runs (around all four bases) for a 100%. Students choose what combination they would like to use to attain that number of runs.

Benefits

Responsibility. With this menu, students still have complete control over their own grades.

Flexibility. This menu allows for many choices at each level. Students should have no trouble finding something that catches their interest.

Theme. This menu has a fun theme that students enjoy and can be used throughout the classroom. A bulletin board can be set up with a baseball diamond, with each student having his or her own player who can move through the bases. Not only can students keep track of their own RBIs, but they can have a visual reminder of what they have completed, as well.

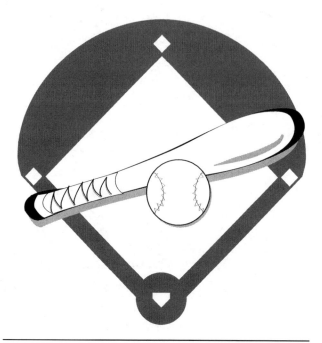

Figure 1.4. Baseball menu.

Limitations

One Topic. This menu is best used for one topic with many objectives for in-depth study.

Preparation. With so many choices available to students, teachers should have all materials ready at the beginning of the unit for students to be able to choose any of the activities on the list. This sometimes is a consideration for space in the classroom.

One Free Choice. This menu also has only one opportunity for free choice for students, in the homerun section.

Time Considerations

These menus are usually intended for a longer amount of completion time, depending on the number of runs required for a 100%. At most, these menus are intended for 4 or 5 weeks.

Game Show Menu

"This menu really challenged my students. If one of my students saw another student choosing a more difficult option, they wanted to choose one, too. I had very few students choose the basic options on this menu. It was wonderful!"

—Sixth-grade science teacher

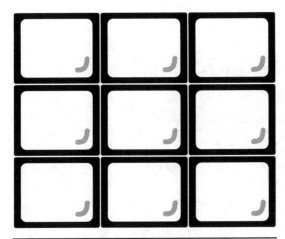

Figure 1.5. Game show menu.

Description

The Game Show menu (see Figure 1.5) is the most complex menu. It covers multiple topics or objectives with at least three predetermined choices and a free student choice for each objective. Choices are assigned points based on the levels of Bloom's Revised taxonomy. All choices carry different weights and have different expectations for completion time and effort. A point criterion is set forth that equals 100%. Students must complete at least one activity from each objective in order to reach their goal.

Benefits

Free Choice. This menu allows many choices for students, but if they do not want to complete the offered activities, they can propose their own activity for each objective.

Responsibility. This menu also allows students to guarantee their own grades.

Different Learning Levels. It also has the flexibility to allow for individualized contracts for different learning levels within the classroom. Each student can contract for a certain number of points for their grade.

Objectives Guaranteed. The teacher is also guaranteed that the students complete an activity from each objective covered, even if it is at a lower level.

Limitations

Confirm Expectations. The only real limitation here is that students (and parents) must understand the guidelines for completing the menu.

Time Considerations

These menus are usually intended for a longer amount of completion time. Although they can be used as a yearlong menu (each column could be a grading period), they are usually intended for 4–6 weeks.

Free Choice

> " . . . the free choice. I love it, love it!!! I got to do what I really wanted to! [The teacher] let me reserch [*sic*] my own book."
>
> —*Second-grade student, when asked what she liked most about the menu students had just completed*

With most of the menus, the students are allowed to submit a free choice for their teacher's consideration. Figure 1.6 shows two sample proposal forms that have been used many times successfully in my classroom. The form used is based on the type of menu being presented. If students are using the Tic-Tac-Toe menu, there is no need to submit a point proposal. A copy of these forms should be given to each student when each menu is first introduced. A discussion should be held with the students so they understand the expectations of a free choice. If students do not want to make a proposal using the proposal form after the teacher has discussed the entire menu and its activities, they can place the unused form in a designated place in the classroom. Others may want to use their form, and it is often surprising who wants to submit a proposal form after hearing about the opportunity!

Proposal forms must be submitted before students begin working on their free-choice products. The teacher then knows what the students are working on and the student knows the expectations the teacher has for that product. Once approved, the forms can easily be stapled to the student's menu sheet. The students can refer to it as they develop their

Name _____   Teacher's Approval: _____

Free-Choice Proposal Form for Point-Based Menu

Points Requested: _____   Points Approved: _____

<u>Proposal Outline</u>

1. What specific topic or idea will you learn about?

2. What criteria should be used to grade it? (Neatness, content, creativity, artistic value, etc.)

3. What will your product look like?

4. What materials will you need from the teacher to create this product?

Name _____   Teacher's Approval: _____

Free-Choice Proposal Form

<u>Proposal Outline</u>

1. What specific topic or idea will you learn about?

2. What criteria should be used to grade it? (Neatness, content, creativity, artistic value, etc.)

3. What will your product look like?

4. What materials will you need from the teacher to create this product?

Figure 1.6. Sample proposal forms for free choice.

free-choice product, and when the grading takes place, the teacher can refer to the agreement for the "graded" features of the product.

Each part of the proposal form is important and needs to be discussed with students:

- *Name/Teacher's Approval.* The student must submit this form to the teacher for approval. The teacher will carefully review all of the information, send it back to the student for correction, if needed, and then sign the top.
- *Points Requested.* Found only on the point-based menu proposal form, this is usually where negotiation needs to take place. Students usually will submit their first request for a very high number (even the 100% goal.) They really do equate the amount of time something will take with the amount of points it should earn. But, please note, the points are *always* based on the levels of Bloom's Revised taxonomy. For example, a PowerPoint presentation with a vocabulary word quiz would get minimal points, although it may have taken a long time to create. If the students have not been exposed to the levels of Bloom's Revised taxonomy, this can be difficult to explain. You can always refer to the popular "Bloom's Verbs" to help explain the difference between time requirements and higher level activities.
- *Points Approved.* Found only on the point-based menu proposal form, this is the final decision recorded by the teacher once the point haggling is finished.
- *Proposal Outline.* This is where the student will tell you everything about the product he or she intends to complete. These questions should be completed in such a way that you can really picture what the student is planning on completing. This also shows you that the student knows what he or she is planning on completing.
  - *What specific topic or idea will you learn about?* Students need to be specific here. It is not acceptable to write *science* or *reading*. This is where they look at the objectives of the project and choose which objective their project demonstrates.
  - *What criteria should be used to grade it?* Although there are rubrics for all of the projects that the students might create, it is important for the students to explain what criteria are most important to evaluate the product. The student may indicate that the rubric being used for all the predetermined projects is fine; however, he or she may also want to add other criteria here.
  - *What will your product look like?* It is important that this be as detailed as possible. If a student cannot express what it will "look

like," he or she has probably not given the free-choice plan enough thought.

- *What materials will you need from the teacher to create this product?* This is an important consideration. Sometimes students do not have the means to purchase items for their project. This can be negotiated, as well, but if you ask what students may need, they often will develop even grander ideas for their free choice.

CHAPTER 2

How to Use Menus in the Classroom

There are different ways to use instructional menus in the classroom. In order to decide how to implement each menu, the following questions should be considered: How much prior knowledge of the topic being taught do the students have before the unit or lesson begins and how much information is readily available for students to obtain on their own?

There are three customary ways to use menus in the classroom. Using them for enrichment and supplementary activities is the most common. In this case, the students usually do not have a lot of background knowledge and the information about the topic may not be readily available to all students. The teacher will introduce the menu and the activities at the beginning of a unit. The teacher will then progress through the content at the normal rate, using his or her own curricular materials and periodically allowing class time and homework time throughout the unit for students to work on their menu choices to supplement a deeper understanding of the lessons being taught. This method is very effective, as it builds in an immediate use for the content the teacher is covering. For example, at the beginning of a unit on fractions, the teacher many introduce the menu with the explanation that students may not have all of the knowledge to complete all of their choices yet. During the unit, however, more content will be provided and they will be prepared to work on new choices.

If students want to work ahead, they certainly can find the information on their own, but that is not required. Gifted students often see this as a challenge and will begin to investigate concepts mentioned in the menu before the teacher discusses them. This helps build an immense pool of background knowledge before the topic is even discussed in the classroom. As teachers, we fight the battle of having students read ahead or "come to class prepared to discuss." By introducing a menu at the beginning of a unit and allowing students to complete products as instruction progresses, the students naturally investigate the information and come to class prepared without it being a completely separate requirement.

Another option for using menus in the classroom is to replace certain curricular activities the teacher uses to teach the specified content. In this case, the students may have some limited background knowledge about the content and information is readily available for them in their classroom resources. The teacher would pick and choose which aspects of the content must be directly taught to the students, and which could be appropriately learned and reinforced through product menus. The unit is then designed using both formal instructional lessons and specific menu days where the students will use the menu to reinforce the prior knowledge they already have learned. In order for this option to be effective, the teacher must feel very comfortable with the students' prior knowledge level. Another variation on this method is using the menus to drive center or station activities. Centers have many different functions in the classroom—most importantly reinforcing the instruction that has taken place. Rather than having a set rotation for centers, the teacher could use the menu activities as enrichment or supplementary activities during center time for those students who need more than just reinforcement; centers could be set up with the materials students would need to complete various products.

The third option for menu use is the use of mini-lessons, with the menus driving the accompanying classroom activities. This method is best used when the majority of the students have a lot of prior knowledge about the topic. The teacher can design 10–15 minute mini-lessons, where students would quickly review basic concepts that are already familiar to them. The students are then turned loose to choose an activity on the menu to show they understand the concept. The game show menu usually works very well with this method of instruction, as the topics across the top usually lend themselves to the mini-lessons. It is important that the students have prior knowledge on the content because the lesson cycle is cut very short in this use of menus. Using menus in this way does not allow teachers to use the guided practice step of the lesson, as it is assumed the students already understand the information. The teacher is simply reviewing the information and then moving right to the higher levels of Bloom's Revised taxonomy by asking students to create a product. By using the menus in this way, the teacher avoids the "I already know this" glossy looks from his or her students. Another important consideration is the independence level of the students. In order for this use of menus to be effective, students will need to be able to work independently for up to 30 minutes after the mini-lesson. Because students are often interested in the product they have chosen, this is not a critical issue, but still one worth mentioning as teachers consider how they would like to use various menus in their classroom.

CHAPTER 3

Guidelines for Products

> ## "Each project is unique."
>
> *—Fifth-grade student, when asked why he enjoys choice menus*

This chapter outlines the different types of products included in the featured menus, as well as the guidelines and expectations for each. It is very important that students know exactly what the expectations of a completed product are when they choose to work on it. By discussing these expectations *before* students begin and having the information readily available ahead of time, you will limit the frustration on everyone's part.

$1 Contract

Consideration should be given to the cost of creating the products featured on any menu. The resources available to students vary within a classroom, and students should not be graded on the amount of materials they can purchase to make a product look better. These menus are designed to equalize the resources students have available. The materi-

---

$1 Contract

I did not spend more than $1.00 on my _____.

_____   _____
               Student Signature   Date

My child, _____, did not spend more than $1.00 on the product he or she created.

_____   _____
               Parent Signature   Date

Figure 3.1. $1 contract.

als for most products are available for less than a dollar and can often be found in a teacher's classroom as part of the classroom supplies. If a product requires materials from the student, there is a $1 contract as part of the product criteria. This is a very important piece in the explanation of the product. First of all, by limiting the amount of money a child can spend, it creates an equal amount of resources for all students. Secondly, it actually encourages a more creative product. When students are limited by the amount of materials they can readily purchase, they often have to use materials from home in new and unique ways. Figure 3.1 is a sample of the contract that has been used many times in my classroom with various products.

The Products

Table 3.1 contains a list of the products used in this book. These products were chosen for their flexibility in meeting learning styles, as well as for being products many teachers are already using in their classroom. They have been arranged by learning style—visual, kinesthetic, or auditory—and each menu has been designed to include products from all of the learning styles. Of course, some of the products may be listed in more than one area depending on how they are presented or implemented. The specific expectations for all of the products are presented in an easy-

Table 3.1
Products

Visual	Kinesthetic	Auditory
Acrostic	Commercial	Commercial
Advertisement	Concentration Cards	Interview
Book Cover	Diorama	News Report
Brochure/Pamphlet	Experiment	Play
Cartoon/Comic Strip	Flipbook	PowerPoint—Presentation
Collage	Game	Puppet
Crossword Puzzle	Mobile	Song/Rap
Greeting Card	Model	Speech
Letter	Play	Student-Taught Lesson
Map	Product Cube	Video
Mind Map	Puppet	You Be the Person Presentation
Newspaper Article	Student-Taught Lesson	
Poster	Video	
PowerPoint—Stand Alone		
Questionnaire		
Recipe/Recipe Card		
Scrapbook		
Story		
Trading Cards		
Venn Diagram		
Video		
Windowpane		
Worksheet		

to-read card format that can be reproduced for students (see Figure 3.2). This format is convenient for students to have in front of them when they work on their projects. These cards also can be laminated and posted on a bulletin board for easy access during classroom work.

Acrostic	Advertisement	Book Cover
• At least 8.5" x 11" • Neatly written or typed • Target word will be written down the left side of the paper • Each descriptive word chosen must begin with one of the letters from the target word • Each descriptive word chosen must be related to the target word	• At least 8.5" x 11" • A slogan should be included • Color picture of item or service • Include price, if appropriate • Can be developed on the computer	• Front Cover—title, author, image • Cover Inside Flap—summary of the book • Back Inside Flap—brief biography of the author • Back Cover—editorial comments about the book • Spine—Title and Author
Brochure/Pamphlet	**Cartoon/Comic Strip**	**Collage**
• At least 8.5" x 11" • Must be in three-fold format; front fold has the title and picture • Must have both pictures and written text • Information should be in paragraph form with at least five facts included	• At least 8.5" x 11" • Should have at least six cells • Must have meaningful dialogue • Must include color	• At least 8.5" x 11" • Pictures must be neatly cut from magazines or newspapers (no clip art) • Label items as required in task
Commercial	**Concentration Cards**	**Crossword Puzzle**
• Must be 5–10 minutes in length • Script must be turned in before play is presented • Can be presented live to an audience or recorded • Props or some form of costume must be used • Can include more than one person	• At least 20 index cards (10 matching sets) must be made • Both pictures and words can be used • Information should be placed on just one side of each card • Include an answer key that shows the matches • All cards must be submitted in a carrying bag	• At least 20 significant words or phrases should be included • Develop appropriate clues • Include puzzle and answer key
Diorama	**Experiment**	**Flipbook**
• At least 4" x 5" x 8" • Must be self-standing • All interior space must be covered with relevant pictures and information • Name written on the back in permanent ink • Informational/title card attached to diorama	• Neatly written or typed • Should include a testable problem, a hypothesis with explanation, a materials list with specific measurements, specific procedures, a data table with units, and a conclusion. • Graphs should be labeled and complete, as well as appropriate for showing the data.	• At least 8.5" x 11" folded in half • All information or opinions are supported by facts • Created with the correct number of flaps cut into the top • Color is optional • Name must be written on the back

Figure 3.2. Product guidelines.

© Prufrock Press Inc. • *Differentiating Instruction With Menus: Math* • *Grades 3–5*
Permission is granted to photocopy or reproduce this page for single classroom use only.

Game	Greeting Card	Interview
• At least four thematic game pieces • At least 25 colored/thematic squares • At least 20 question/activity cards • Include a thematic title on the board • Include a complete set of rules for playing the game • At least the size of an open file folder (11" x 17")	• Front—colored pictures, words optional • Front Inside—personal note related to topic • Back Inside—greeting or saying; must meet product criteria • Back Outside—logo, publisher, and price for card	• Must have at least five questions relevant to the topic being studied • Questions and answers must be neatly written or typed
Letter	**Map**	**Mind Map**
• Neatly written or typed • Uses proper letter format • At least three paragraphs in length • Must follow type of letter stated in the menu (e.g., friendly, persuasive, informational)	• At least 8.5" x 11" • Accurate information is included • Includes at least 10 relevant locations • Includes compass rose, legend, scale, and key	• At least 8.5" x 11" paper • Must have one central idea • Follow the "no more than four" rule—no more than four words coming from any one word
Mobile	**Model**	**News Report**
• At least 10 pieces of related information • Includes color and pictures • Has at least three layers of hanging information • Hangs in a balanced way	• At least 8" x 8" x 12" • Parts of model must be labeled • Should be in scale when appropriate • Must include a title card • Name written on model in ink	• Must address the who, what, where, when, why, and how of the topic • Script of report turned in with project, or before if performance will be "live" • Must be either performed live or recorded
Newspaper Article	**Play**	**Poster**
• Must be informational in nature • Must follow standard newspaper format • Must include picture with caption that supports article • At least three paragraphs in length • Neatly written or typed	• Must be between 5–10 minutes long • Script must be turned in before play is presented • Must be presented to an audience • Should have props or some form of costume • Can include more than one person	• Should be the size of a standard poster board • Includes at least five pieces of important information • Must have title • Must contain both words and pictures • Name must be written on the back

Figure 3.2. Product guidelines.

PowerPoint—Presentation	PowerPoint—Stand Alone	Product Cube
• At least 10 informational slides and one title slide with student's name • Slides must have color and at least one graphic per page • Animation is optional, and should not distract from information being presented • Presentation should be timed and flow with the oral presentation	• Should have at least 10 informational slides and one title slide with student's name • Limit each slide to 15–20 words • Slides must have color and at least one graphic per page • Animation is optional, and should not distract from information being presented	• All six sides of the cube must be filled with information • Name must be printed neatly at the bottom of one of the sides of the cube
Puppet	**Questionnaire**	**Recipe/Recipe Card**
• Puppet should be handmade and must have a moveable mouth • A list of supplies used to make the puppet must be turned in with the puppet • If used in a play, all play criteria must be met, as well.	• Neatly written or typed • Includes at least 10 questions with possible answers • At least one question that requires a written response • Questions must be helpful to gathering information on the topic being studied	• Must be written neatly or typed on a piece of paper or an index card • Must have a list of ingredients with measurements for each • Must have numbered steps that explain how to make the recipe
Scrapbook	**Song/Rap**	**Speech**
• Cover of scrapbook must have a meaningful title and the student's name • Must have at least five themed pages • Each page will have at least one picture • All photos will have captions	• Words must make sense • Can be presented to an audience or taped • Written words will be turned in before performance or with taped song • Should be at least 2 minutes in length	• Must be at least 2 minutes in length • Should not be read from written paper • Note cards can be used • Written speech must be turned in before speech is presented • Voice must be clear, loud, and easy to understand
Story	**Trading Cards**	**Venn Diagram**
• Must be neatly written or typed • Must have all of the elements of a well-written story (setting, characters, problem, events, and solution) • Must be appropriate length to allow for story elements	• Includes at least 10 cards • Each card should be at least 3" x 5" • Each should have a colored picture • Includes at least three facts on the subject of the card • Cards must have information on both sides • All cards must be submitted in a carrying bag	• At least 8.5" x 11" • Shapes should be thematic and neatly drawn • Must have a title for the entire diagram and a title for each section • Must have at least six items in each section of the diagram • Name must be written on the back of the paper

Figure 3.2. Product guidelines.

© Prufrock Press Inc. • *Differentiating Instruction With Menus: Math • Grades 3–5*
Permission is granted to photocopy or reproduce this page for single classroom use only.

Video	Windowpane	Worksheet
• Must be recorded • Turn in a written plan or story board with project • Students will need to arrange their own video recorder or allow teacher at least 3 days notice for use of video recorder • Covers important information about the project • Name must be written on video or disc	• At least 8.5" x 11" • At least six squares • Each square must include both a picture and words • Name should be recorded on the bottom righthand corner of the front of the windowpane	• Must be 8.5" x 11" • Neatly written or typed • Must cover the specific topic or question in detail • Must be creative in design • Must have at least one graphic • An answer key will be turned in with the worksheet
You Be the Person Presentation • Take on the role of the person • Cover at least five important facts about his or her life • Presentation should be 3–5 minutes in length • Script must be turned in prior to the presentation • Should be prepared to answer questions from the audience while in character • Must have props or a costume		

Figure 3.2. Product guidelines.

© Prufrock Press Inc. • *Differentiating Instruction With Menus: Math • Grades 3–5*
Permission is granted to photocopy or reproduce this page for single classroom use only.

CHAPTER 4

Rubrics

"All the grading of the projects kept me from using menus before. The rubric makes it easier though and they [the different projects] are fun to see."

—Fourth-grade teacher,
when asked to explain reservations about using menus

The most common reason teachers feel uncomfortable with menus is the need for fair and equal grading. Teachers often feel it is easier to grade the same type of product made by all of the students, rather than grading a large number of different products, none of which looks like any other. The great equalizer for hundreds of different products is a generic rubric that can cover all of the important qualities of an excellent product.

All-Purpose Rubric

Figure 4.1 is an example of a rubric that has been classroom tested with various menus. This rubric can be used with any point value activity

Name:_____

All-Purpose Product Rubric

Criteria	Excellent Full Credit	Good Half Credit	Poor No Credit	Self
Content: Is the content of the product well chosen?	Content chosen represents the best choice for the product. Graphics are well chosen and related to content.	Information or graphics are related to content, but are not the best choice for the product.	Information or graphics presented does not appear to be related to topic or task.	
Completeness: Is everything included in the product?	All information needed is included. Product meets the product criteria and the criteria of the task as stated.	Some important information is missing. Product meets the product criteria and the criteria of the task as stated.	Most important information is missing. The product does not meet the task, or does not meet the product criteria.	
Creativity: Is the product original?	Presentation of information is from a new perspective. Graphics are original. Product includes an element of fun and interest.	Presentation of information is from a new perspective. Graphics are not original. Product has elements of fun and interest.	There is no evidence of new thoughts or perspectives in the product.	
Correctness: Is all the information included correct?	All information presented in the product is correct and accurate.	N/A	Any portion of the information presented in the product is incorrect.	
Appropriate Communication: Is the information in the product well communicated?	All information is neat and easy to read. Product is in appropriate format and shows significant effort. Oral presentations are easy to understand and presented with fluency.	Most of the product is neat and easy to read. Product is in appropriate format and shows significant effort. Oral presentations are easy to understand, with some fluency.	The product is not neat and easy to read or the product is not in the appropriate format. It does not show significant effort. Oral presentation was not fluent or easy to understand.	
			Total Grade:	

Figure 4.1. All-purpose product rubric.

© Prufrock Press Inc. • *Differentiating Instruction With Menus: Math • Grades 3–5*
Permission is granted to photocopy or reproduce this page for single classroom use only.

presented in a menu. When a menu is presented to students, this rubric can be reproduced on the back of the menu with its guidelines. It can also be given to students to keep in their folder with their product cards so they always know the expectations as they complete projects throughout the school year. The first time students see this rubric, it should be explained in detail, especially the last column, titled *Self*. It is very important that students self-evaluate their projects. This column can provide a unique perspective of the project as it is being graded. Note: This rubric was designed to be specific enough that students will know the criteria the teacher is seeking, but general enough that they can still be as creative as they like in the creation of their product.

Student-Taught Lessons and Student Presentation Rubrics

Although the generic rubric can be used for all activities, there are two occasions that seem to warrant a special rubric: student-taught lessons and student presentations. These are unique situations, with many fine details that should be considered separately.

Teachers often would like to allow students to teach their fellow classmates, but are not comfortable with the grading aspect of the assignment. The student-taught lesson rubric (see Figure 4.2) helps focus the student on the important aspects of a well-designed lesson, and allows teachers to make the evaluation a little more subjective. The student-taught lesson rubric included for these menus is appropriate for all levels, including third grade.

Another area that can be difficult to evaluate is student presentations. The first consideration is that of objectivity. The objectivity can be addressed through a very specific presentation rubric that states the expectations for the speaker. The rubric will need to be discussed and various criteria demonstrated before the students begin preparing presentations. The second consideration is that of the audience and its interest. How frustrating it can be to have to grade 30 presentations when the audience is not paying attention, off task, or tuning out. This can be solved by allowing your audience to be directly involved in the presentation. All of the students have been instructed on the oral presentation rubric (see Figure 4.3), so when they receive their own rubric to give feedback to their classmates, they are quite comfortable with the criteria.

Student-Taught Lesson Grading Rubric

Name _____

Parts of Lesson	Excellent	Good	Fair	Poor	Self
Prepared and Ready: All materials and lesson ready at start of class period, from warm-up to conclusion of lesson.	10 Everything is ready to present.	6 Lesson is present, but small amount of scrambling.	3 Lesson is present, but major scrambling.	0 No lesson ready or missing major components.	
Understanding: Presenter understands the material well. Students understand information presented.	20 Presenter understands; almost all of the students understand information.	12 Presenter understands; 25% of students do not.	4 Presenter understands; 50% of students do not.	0 Presenter is confused.	
Completion: Includes all significant information from section or topic.	15 Includes all important information.	10 Includes most important information.	2 Includes less than 50% of the important information.	0 Information is not related.	
Practice: Includes some way for students to practice or access the information.	20 Practice present, well chosen.	10 Practice present, can be applied effectively.	5 Practice present, not related or best choice.	0 No practice or students are confused.	
Interest/Fun: Most of the class involved, interested, and participating.	15 Everyone interested and participating.	10 75% actively participating.	5 Less than 50% actively participating.	0 Everyone off task.	
Creativity: Information presented in imaginative way.	20 Wow, creative! I never would have thought of that!	12 Good ideas!	5 Some good pieces but general instruction.	0 No creativity; all lecture/ notes/ worksheet.	
				Total Grade:	

Your Topic/Objective:

Comments:

Don't Forget:
All copy requests and material requests must be made at least 24 hours in advance.

Figure 4.2. Student-taught lesson grading rubric.

© Prufrock Press Inc. • *Differentiating Instruction With Menus: Math • Grades 3–5*
Permission is granted to photocopy or reproduce this page for single classroom use only.

Students are asked to rank their classmates on a scale of 1–10 in the areas of content, flow, and the prop they chose to enhance their presentation (see Figure 4.4). They are also asked to state two things the presenter did well. Although most students understand this should be a positive experience for the presenter, it may want to be reinforced that some notes are not necessary on their peer rankings; for example, if the presenter dropped their product and had to pick it up, the presenter knows this and it probably does not need to be noted again. The feedback should be positive and specific, as well. A comment of "Great!" is not what should be recorded; instead, something specific such as "I could hear you speak loudly and clearly throughout the entire presentation," or "You had great graphics!" should be written on the form. These types of comments really make the students take note and feel great about their presentations. The teacher should not be surprised to note that the students often look through all of their classmates' feedback and comments before ever consulting the rubric the teacher completed. Once students have completed a feedback form for a presenter, the forms can then be gathered at the end of each presentation, stapled together, and given to the presenter at the end of the class.

Name:_____

Oral Presentation Rubric

	Excellent	Good	Fair	Poor	Self
Content— Complete The presentation included everything it should.	**30** Presentation included all of the important information about the topic being presented.	**20** Presentation covered most of the important information, but one key idea was missing.	**10** Presentation covered some of the important information, but more than one key idea was missing.	**0** Presentation included some information, but it was trivial or fluff.	
Content—Correct All of the information presented was accurate.	**30** All of the information presented was accurate.	**20** All of the information presented was correct with a few unintentional errors that were quickly corrected.	**10** Most of the information presented was correct, but there were a few errors	**0** The information presented was not correct.	
Content— Consistency Speaker stayed on topic during the presentation.	**10** Presenter stayed on topic 100% of the time.	**7** Presenter stayed on topic 90–99% of the time.	**4** Presenter stayed on topic 80–89% of the time.	**0** It was hard to tell what the topic was.	
Prop Speaker had at least one prop that was directly related to the presentation.	**20** Presenter had the prop and it complimented the presentation.	**12** Presenter had a prop, but it was not the best choice.	**4** Presenter had a prop, but there was no clear reason for its choice.	**0** No prop.	
Flow Speaker knew the presentation well, so the words were well-spoken and flowed well together.	**10** Presentation flowed well. Speaker did not stumble over words.	**7** Some flow problems, but they did not distract from information.	**4** Some flow problems interrupted presentation; presenter seemed flustered.	**0** Constant flow problems; information was not presented in a way it could be understood.	
				Total Grade:	

Figure 4.3. Oral presentation rubric.

© Prufrock Press Inc. • *Differentiating Instruction With Menus: Math • Grades 3–5*
Permission is granted to photocopy or reproduce this page for single classroom use only.

Topic: _____ Student's Name_____

On a scale of 1–10, rate the following areas:

	Your Ranking	
Content (Depth of information. How well did the speaker know his or her information? Was the information correct? Could the speaker answer questions?)	☐	Give one specific reason why you gave this number.
Flow (Did the presentation flow smoothly? Did the speaker appear confident and ready to speak?)	☐	Give one specific reason why you gave this number.
Prop (Did the speaker explain the prop he or she chose? Did the choice seem logical? Was it the best choice?)	☐	Give one specific reason why you gave this number.

Comments: Below, write two specific things that you think the presenter did well.

Topic: _____ Student's Name_____

On a scale of 1–10, rate the following areas:

	Your Ranking	
Content (Depth of information. How well did the speaker know his or her information? Was the information correct? Could the speaker answer questions?)	☐	Give one specific reason why you gave this number.
Flow (Did the presentation flow smoothly? Did the speaker appear confident and ready to speak?)	☐	Give one specific reason why you gave this number.
Prop (Did the speaker explain the prop he or she chose? Did the choice seem logical? Was it the best choice?)	☐	Give one specific reason why you gave this number.

Comments: Below, write two specific things that you think the presenter did well.

Figure 4.4. Student feedback rubric.

© Prufrock Press Inc. • *Differentiating Instruction With Menus: Math • Grades 3–5*
Permission is granted to photocopy or reproduce this page for single classroom use only.

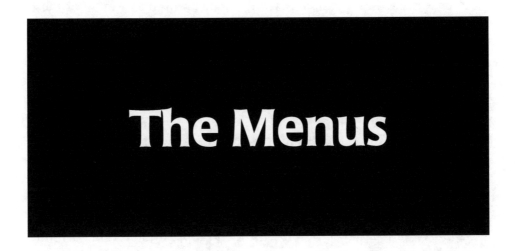

The Menus

How to Use the Menu Pages

Each menu in this section has:
- an introduction page for the teacher,
- the content menu,
- any specific guidelines, and
- activities mentioned in the menu.

Introduction Pages

The introduction pages are meant to provide an overview of each menu. They are divided into five areas.

1. *Objectives covered through the menu and activities.* This area will list all of the objectives that the menu can address. Menus are arranged in such a way that if students complete the guidelines set forth in the instructions for the menu, all of these objectives will be covered.

2. *Materials needed by students for completion.* For each menu, it is expected that the teacher will provide or students will have access to the following materials: lined paper; glue; crayons, colored pen-

cils, or markers; and blank 8 ½" by 11" white paper. The introduction page also includes a list of additional materials that may be needed by students. Students do have the choice about the menu items they can complete, so it is possible that the teacher will not need all of these materials for every student.

3. *Special notes.* Some menus allow students to choose to present demonstrations, experiments, songs, or PowerPoint presentations to their classmates. This section will give any special tips on managing these student presentations. This section will also share any tips to consider for a specific activity.

4. *Time frame.* Most menus are best used in at least a one-week time frame. Some are better suited to more than 2 weeks. This section will give you an overview about the best time frame for completing the entire menu, as well as options for shorter time periods. If teachers do not have time to devote to an entire menu, they can certainly choose the 1–2-day option for any menu topic students are currently studying.

5. *Suggested forms.* This is a list of the rubrics that should be available for students as the menus are introduced. If a menu has a free-choice option, the appropriate proposal form will also be listed here.

CHAPTER 5

Whole Numbers and Operations

Place Value

List Menu

Objectives Covered Through This Menu and These Activities

- Students will be able to find the place value of integers in a five-digit number.
- Students will be able to gain an understanding of larger numbers.
- Students will be able to locate and analyze how larger numbers are used in our everyday world.

Materials Needed by Students for Completion

- *How Much Is a Million?* by David M. Schwartz
- Poster board or large white paper
- Newspapers
- Coat hangers (for mobile)
- Index cards (for mobile)
- String (for mobile)
- Blank index cards

Time Frame

- 1–2 weeks—Students are given the menu as the unit is started and the guidelines and point expectations are discussed. Because this menu covers one topic in depth, the teacher will go over all of the options on the menu and have students place check marks in the boxes next to the activities they are most interested in completing. As instruction continues, the activities are completed by students and submitted for grading.
- 1–2 days—The teacher chooses an activity from an objective to use with the entire class during that lesson time.

Suggested Forms

- All-purpose rubric
- Proposal form for point-based projects

Name:_____

Place Value

Guidelines:

1. You may complete as many of the activities listed as you would like within the time period given.
2. You may choose any combination of activities.
3. Your goal is 100 points. You may earn up to _____ points in extra credit.
4. You may be as creative as you like within the guidelines listed below.
5. You must show your plan to your teacher by _____.
6. Activities may be turned in at any time during the working time period. They will be graded and recorded on this sheet as you continue to work, so keep it safe!

Plan to Do	Activity to Complete	Point Value	Date Completed	Points Earned
	Find the populations of five cities in your state. Put them in order from least to greatest.	15		
	Think of 2 four- or five-digit mystery numbers. Write clues for your classmates to try and discover each number. Be creative when you use place value in your clues.	25		
	Read the book *How Much is Million?* Choose your own item and calculate how much space it would take to reach a million.	25		
	If you had a million dollars to spend, what would you buy? Create a list with the cost of each item showing how you would spend the money.	25		
	Make a set of cards with the numbers 1 through 9 on them. Using only those cards, create a set of activities that would test your classmates on their knowledge of place value.	20		
	Create a mobile to represent the population of your state. For each number, give its place value.	15		
	Research the distance of the planets in the solar system from Earth. Make a chart that lists the planets and their distances in order from farthest to closest.	20		
	Look at a newspaper from this week. Find the largest number in the paper. Cut out the article and attach it to a poster, and list all the place values for the number.	15		
	Create a set of trading cards for each place value. Be creative in the facts you record about each.	20		
	Choose a page without any pictures in one of your textbooks. Develop a method to calculate the number of words on that page without counting them all. Test your theory on other pages in the book.	25		
	Free choice: Must be outlined on a proposal form and approved before beginning work.			
	Total number of points you are planning to earn.		**Total points earned:**	

I am planning to complete _____ activities that could earn up to a total of _____ points.

Teacher's initials _____ Student's signature _____

Integers

2-5-8 Menu

Objectives Covered Through This Menu and These Activities

- Students will be able to correctly arrange integers on a number line.
- Students will be able to give real-world examples of positive and negative integers.
- Students will understand how to make calculations with positive and negative integers.

Materials Needed by Students for Completion

- Poster board or large white paper
- Cube template (for integers cube)

Time Frame

- 1–2 weeks—Students are given the menu as the unit is started, and the teacher discusses all of the product options on the menu. As the different options are discussed, students will choose products that add to a total of 10 points. As the lessons progress through the week, the teacher and the students should refer back to the options associated with the content being taught.
- 1–2 days—The teacher chooses an activity from the menu to use with the entire class.

Suggested Forms

- All-purpose rubric
- Proposal form for point-based projects

Name:_____

Integers

Directions: Choose two activities from the menu below. The activities must total 10 points. Place a check mark in each box to show which activities you will complete. All activities must be completed by

_____.

---

2 Points

☐ Create an interactive number line with at least five positive and five negative integers. Your number line should allow users to put the numbers in the correct location and check to see if they are right.

☐ Make a poster that shows at least 10 occasions when negative integers are used.

---

5 Points

☐ Create a song that tells a sad story based around a negative integer and its impact on someone's life.

☐ Create an advertisement for a product in which integers play an important role.

☐ Create a brochure that shows how to handle integers and do calculations with them.

☐ Create an integer cube. Each side should have a real-world integer word problem for your classmates to solve.

---

8 Points

☐ You are a doctor who just graduated from college. You currently owe $105,000 for your education. You will only make about $50,000 a year for the first 5 years. Create a budget that could get you out of debt as quickly as possible. Take into account all the normal living costs you would encounter in one year.

☐ Free choice—Prepare a proposal form and submit to your teacher for approval.

Integers Cube

Complete the cube for integers. Use this pattern or create your own cube. Each side of the cube should have a real-world integer word problem for your classmates to solve. Be creative, but remember that your problem should be something that could happen!

© Prufrock Press Inc. • *Differentiating Instruction With Menus: Math • Grades 3–5*
Permission is granted to photocopy or reproduce this page for single classroom use only.

Prime and Composite Numbers

2-5-8 Menu

Objective Covered Through This Menu and These Activities

- Students will be able to distinguish between prime and composite numbers.

Materials Needed by Students for Completion

- 100s chart
- List of products
- Large index cards (for rule cards)
- Instructions for making a dichotomous key (see How to Make a Dichotomous Key)

Special Notes on the Use of This Menu

This menu does offer the option to create a dichotomous key. Some students may or may not have had experience creating one. There is an instruction sheet with examples (see How to Make a Dichotomous Key), although the key students create will be much more detailed.

Time Frame

- 1–2 weeks—Students are given the menu as the unit is started, and the teacher discusses all of the product options on the menu. As the different options are discussed, students will choose products that add to a total of 10 points. As the lessons progress through the week, the teacher and the students should refer back to the options associated with the content being taught.
- 1–2 days—The teacher chooses an activity from the menu to use with the entire class.

Suggested Forms

- All-purpose rubric
- Proposal form for point-based projects

Name:_____

Prime and Composite Numbers

Directions: Choose two activities from the menu below. The activities must total 10 points. Place a check mark in each box to show which activities you will complete. All activities must be completed by

_____.

---

2 Points

❒ Fill in a 100s chart, color coding the prime and composite numbers.

❒ Create a themed product that shows the first 10 prime numbers.

---

5 Points

❒ Write a journal entry about either a prime or composite number and its feelings about its fact families.

❒ Create a rule card that lists all the ways to check if a large number is prime or composite.

❒ Create a song or rap that would help your classmates remember the difference between prime and composite numbers.

❒ Free choice—Prepare a proposal form and submit to your teacher for approval.

---

8 Points

❒ Create your own dichotomous key or flow chart that tells the steps to determine if a number is prime or composite. Try and find the fewest steps to guarantee your answer.

❒ Crisis has struck. The number 8 has suddenly disappeared. All of the numbers in his fact family, as well as the numbers he is a part of, have gotten together to try and search for him. Make an attendance list that tells the relationship to 8 for all the numbers who will join the search.

© Prufrock Press Inc. • *Differentiating Instruction With Menus: Math • Grades 3–5*
Permission is granted to photocopy or reproduce this page for single classroom use only.

Name:_____

How to Make a Dichotomous Key

Dichotomous keys are designed to ask questions of the user and eventually lead to a final answer as the user makes decisions. There are different ways to organize these questions. They can be designed in a flow chart design or be a simple list of questions. In order to design a dichotomous key, you want to start asking questions from broad to specific, so users will find their answers.

Let's say that a group of high school students have come to present a play for your class and you do not know their names. A dichotomous key would help you discover their names based on what you observe about the students. Below are two different examples of the same information in the two different kinds of keys. Using the information in the dichotomous keys, see if you can figure out the name of each high school student.

Dichotomous Keys: Flow Chart

The following page shows an example of a dichotomous key flow chart. This type of key uses arrows, which allow the user to follow a path to an unknown object. You would start with the very general question: Is the unknown person a boy or girl? If he is a boy, you will continue on the "boy" path to try and discover the name of the group member. If the person is a girl, your path is a lot shorter. This group only has one girl.

Dichotomous Keys: Question List

This type of key asks questions to help students try and identify an unknown object. The first question is very general

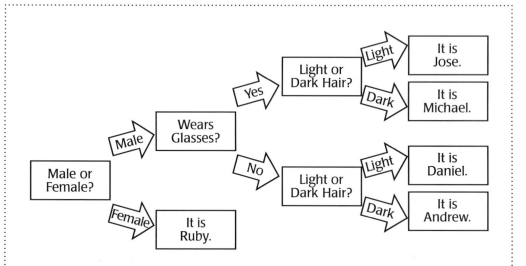

and usually splits the group into two smaller groups. For this key, you will want to know first if the student you are trying to identify is a boy or a girl. From that point on, the questions get more specific.

1. Is the unknown person male or female? If male, go to 2. If female, go to 6.
2. Male: Does he wear glasses? If yes, go to 3. If no, go to 4.
3. Does he have light or dark hair? If light, go to 8. If dark, go to 9.
4. Does he have light or dark hair? If light, go to 5. If dark, go to 7.
5. It is Daniel.
6. It is Ruby.
7. It is Andrew.
8. It is Jose.
9. It is Michael.

How did you do with your identification of the students?

© Prufrock Press Inc. • *Differentiating Instruction With Menus: Math • Grades 3–5*
Permission is granted to photocopy or reproduce this page for single classroom use only.

Coordinate Graphs

2-5-8 Menu

Objectives Covered Through This Menu and These Activities

- Students will be able to plot points on a coordinate graph.
- Students will understand uses for coordinate graphs in our daily lives.

Materials Needed by Students for Completion

- Poster board or large white paper
- Graph paper
- Materials for board games (folders, colored cards, etc.)
- Different maps, including state maps

Special Notes on the Use of This Menu

Two of the activities call for students to use local maps and state maps. These can usually be obtained free of charge through a local travel bureau or a local AAA agency.

Time Frame

- 1–2 weeks—Students are given the menu as the unit is started, and the teacher discusses all of the product options on the menu. As the different options are discussed, students will choose products that add to a total of 10 points. As the lessons progress through the week, the teacher and the students should refer back to the options associated with the content being taught.
- 1–2 days—The teacher chooses an activity from the menu to use with the entire class.

Suggested Forms

- All-purpose rubric
- Proposal form for point-based projects

Coordinate Graphs

Directions: Choose two activities from the menu below. The activities must total 10 points. Place a check mark in each box to show which activities you will complete. All activities must be completed by _____.

---

2 Points

❒ Create a brochure that shows how to plot points and read coordinate graphs.

❒ Make a quiz (or worksheet) for your classmates that tests their ability to plot and recognize points on a graph.

---

5 Points

❒ Using a piece of graph paper, make a drawing. Write instructions telling how to have other students create your drawing using only coordinates.

❒ Develop a game that you could play with friends. It has to have coordinates to move forward in the game.

❒ Create a poster that shows at least five uses of coordinate graphs in our daily lives.

❒ Free choice—Prepare a proposal form and submit to your teacher for approval.

---

8 Points

❒ Maps are divided into areas. You can use the coordinates labeled to find different cities. After examining different maps, make a map of your school and playground with different points of interest and their coordinates. List the points and their location in a legend.

❒ Design a scavenger hunt on our state map. Make up fun questions and riddles that can only be answered by visiting the coordinates you state in the hunt. Be creative in its design. Challenge your classmates with finding at least 15 items.

© Prufrock Press Inc. • *Differentiating Instruction With Menus: Math • Grades 3–5*
Permission is granted to photocopy or reproduce this page for single classroom use only.

Money

Tic-Tac-Toe Menu

Objectives Covered Through This Menu and These Activities

- Students will be able to create different combinations of coins.
- Students will be able to complete calculations with money.
- Students will be able to analyze the saving and spending of money in everyday situations.

Materials Needed by Students for Completion

- Poster board or large white paper
- Materials for board games (folders, colored cards, etc.)
- Materials for student created models

Time Frame

- 2 weeks—Students are given the menu as the unit is started. As the teacher presents lessons throughout the week, he or she refers back to the options associated with that content. The teacher will go over all of the options for that content and have students place check marks in the boxes which represent the activities they are most interested in completing. As teaching continues throughout the 2 weeks, the activities chosen and completed should make a column or a row. When students make this pattern, they have completed one activity on saving money, one activity on different coin combinations, and one problem-solving activity using money.
- 1 week—At the start of the unit, the teacher chooses the three activities he or she feels are most valuable for the students. Stations can be set up in the classroom. These three activities are available for student choice throughout the week, as regular instruction takes place.
- 1–2 days—The teacher chooses an activity from the menu to use with the entire class.

Suggested Forms

- All-purpose rubric
- Proposal form for projects

Money

☐ Change Counting Machines There are machines that will count your change for you, but they charge a 9-cents-per-dollar fee. Is this fee worth it? What is the minimum amount of coins you would turn in (how many coins you think this fee would be worth paying for)? Prepare a speech on the advantages and disadvantages of these machines. Include specific examples and calculations.	**☐ Thanks, Aunt Kay!** For your birthday each year, one of your relatives has decided to give you $10 times your age that year (for example, $50 for your fifth birthday). If all of this money goes into your savings account, will you be able to afford a car by the time you get your drivers license? Show your results.	**☐ Combinations of Money** Your little sister has been saving her money for a year now. She wants to take it all to the bank and trade it in for dollar bills. Create a poster to show her all of the different combinations of the coins that could make $1.00.
☐ The Next Sensation? You have a great idea for a new board game. It will be based on saving and spending money, and will even have a bank. Develop this game and bring it to class for your classmates to play.	**☐ Free Choice** (Fill out your proposal form before beginning the free choice!)	**☐ The Perfect Party** Your parents have promised you a fabulous birthday party. However, you must be able to invite, feed, and entertain all your friends for less than $200. Develop your plan for having your party and staying within the budget.
☐ Combinations of Money Mr. Monie has been saving change his entire life. The time has come for him to pay his electric bill this month, and he doesn't have any dollar bills. He decides he wouldn't mind spending nickels and pennies, but nothing else. If his electric bill is $152, propose two options for him to pay his bill.	**☐ Making the Teachers Happy** You have been given the task of designing a new teacher's lounge for your school. Talk to your teachers to find out what they feel should be included. Create a model that shows how you would like it to look, and total the amount of money that it would take to create the teachers' ultimate lounge.	**☐ Winning Millions?** You have created a television show in which participants can win money based on answering questions correctly. Each time they answer a question correctly, their money doubles. If they start with just one dollar, how many questions will they need to answer correctly to be millionaires? Prepare a poster that shows participants how they can win $1 million.

Check the boxes you plan to complete. They should form a tic-tac-toe across or down. All products are due by: _____.

© Prufrock Press Inc. • *Differentiating Instruction With Menus: Math* • Grades 3–5
Permission is granted to photocopy or reproduce this page for single classroom use only.

Adding and Subtracting Decimals
2-5-8 Menu

Objectives Covered Through This Menu and These Activities
• Students will be able to add and subtract decimals.
• Students will be able to give examples of decimals in the real world.

Materials Needed by Students for Completion
• Poster board or large white paper
• Materials for student created lessons
• Newspapers
• Blank index cards (for card game)

Special Notes on the Use of This Menu
This menu contains an activity that will require the support of the school librarian. The students are asked to find all of the books in the library about math and add their Dewey decimals together. If time is a consideration, the librarian could pull certain books that focus on math and have them placed in a special spot in the library so students could easily locate them and record the numbers.

Time Frame
• 1–2 weeks—Students are given the menu as the unit is started, and the teacher discusses all the product options on the menu. As the different options are discussed, students will choose products that add to a total of 10 points. As the lessons progress through the week, the teacher and the students should refer back to the options associated with the content being taught.
• 1–2 days—The teacher chooses an activity from the menu to use with the entire class.

Suggested Forms
• All-purpose rubric
• Student-taught lesson rubric
• Proposal form for point-based projects

Name:_____

Adding and Subtracting Decimals

Directions: Choose two activities from the menu below. The activities must total 10 points. Place a check mark in each box to show which activities you will complete. All activities must be completed by

_____.

---

2 Points

❒ Create a worksheet for your classmates to help them practice adding and subtracting decimals.

❒ Create a flipbook with examples of adding and subtracting decimals on the flaps with the answers inside.

---

5 Points

❒ Choose a sport of your choice. Prepare a poster that explains how statistics are calculated for that sport. Share examples in your explanation.

❒ Library books can be located by the Dewey decimal numbers on their spine. Just for fun, your school librarian has offered a prize for the first student who can tell her the total of all of the Dewey decimal numbers on the books about math. A student has turned in the answer, but you have been given the assignment to check the answer. On a poster, show the books you have found and how you calculated the correct answer.

❒ Create a concentration card game to match decimal word problems with their answers.

❒ Decimals are big news! Go through two sections of your newspaper and locate all of the numbers recorded as decimals. Estimate the total of all of the numbers, and then calculate it.

---

8 Points

❒ Create a lesson to teach your class how to add and subtract decimals.

❒ Free choice—Prepare a proposal form and submit it to your teacher for approval.

© Prufrock Press Inc. • *Differentiating Instruction With Menus: Math • Grades 3–5*
Permission is granted to photocopy or reproduce this page for single classroom use only.

Decimals

List Menu

Objectives Covered Through This Menu and These Activities

- Students will be able to multiply and divide decimals.
- Students will be able to add and subtract decimals.
- Students will be able to show real-world examples of calculations with decimals.
- Students will be able to identify relationships between fractions and decimals.

Materials Needed by Students for Completion

- Graph paper or Internet access (for crossword puzzle)
- Cube template
- Microsoft PowerPoint or other slideshow software
- Recipes from recipe books
- Blank index cards (for card game)

Time Frame

- 1–2 weeks—Students are given the menu as the unit is started and the guidelines and point expectations on the menu are discussed. Because this menu covers one topic in depth, the teacher will go over all the options for the topic being covered and have students place check marks in the boxes next to the activities they are most interested in completing. As instruction continues, the activities are completed by students and submitted for grading.
- 1–2 days—The teacher chooses an activity from an objective to use with the entire class during the lesson time.

Suggested Forms

- All-purpose rubric
- Proposal form for point-based projects

Name:_____

Decimals

Guidelines:
1. You may complete as many of the activities listed as you would like within the time period given.
2. You may choose any combination of activities.
3. Your goal is 100 points. You may earn up to _____ points extra credit.
4. You may be as creative as you like within the guidelines listed below.
5. You must show your plan to your teacher by _____.
6. Activities may be turned in at any time during the working time period. They will be graded and recorded on this sheet as you continue to work, so keep it safe!

Plan to Do	Activity to Complete	Point Value	Date Completed	Points Earned
	Create a cube game using three cubes. In this game, the players will roll two dice to get decimal numbers and one die to get the mathematical function they must complete. Provide an answer card for all of the possible combinations.	30		
	Write a letter to your parents about how decimals are part of our daily life. Include examples to prove your point.	25		
	Create a set of trading cards for all of the decimals in the eighths family. Include their equivalent fractions, facts about them, and at least one drawing.	25		
	Create a PowerPoint presentation that shows how to add, subtract, multiply, and divide decimals.	25		
	Create a project cube with real-world examples of adding, subtracting, multiplying, and dividing decimals.	20		
	Convert one of your favorite recipes from fractions into decimals. If you needed to prepare the recipe for your class, how much of each ingredient would you need?	20		
	Create a book cover for a math book entitled *Decimals in Our Daily Lives*.	25		
	Create a decimal crossword puzzle in which all of the answers are written in words and all of the clues are problems.	30		
	Create a set of concentration cards to match decimals with their equivalent fractions.	20		
	Make a Venn diagram to compare decimals and fractions.	25		
	Create a number path starting with the number 13.56 and ending with 92.41. Your path must have at least seven steps, and include addition, subtraction, and multiplication. Show your path on a poster.	30		
	Free choice: Must be outlined on a proposal form and approved before beginning work.	10–30		
	Total number of points you are planning to earn.		**Total points earned:**	

I am planning to complete _____ activities that could earn up to a total of _____ points.

Teacher's initials _____ Student's signature _____

© Prufrock Press Inc. • *Differentiating Instruction With Menus: Math • Grades 3–5*
Permission is granted to photocopy or reproduce this page for single classroom use only.

Decimals Cube

Complete the cube for decimals. Use this pattern or create your own cube. Each side of the cube should include real-world examples of adding, subtracting, multiplying, and dividing decimals.

Whole Numbers

Baseball Menu

Objectives Covered Through This Menu and These Activities

- Students will be able to add and subtract whole numbers.
- Students will be able to multiply and divide whole numbers.
- Students will be able to solve problems with whole numbers.
- Students will be able to show how mathematics is used in our daily lives.

Materials Needed by Students for Completion

- Poster board or large white paper
- Graph paper or Internet access (for crossword puzzle)
- Materials for board games (folders, colored cards, etc.)
- Microsoft PowerPoint or other slideshow software
- Blank index cards (for card game and trading cards)
- Cube template
- Materials for student-created lessons
- Advertisements from local grocery stores
- Video camera (for educational video)

Special Notes on the Use of This Menu

This menu allows students to create their own educational video. You may want to plan class time for activity work on this menu, or these students may need to schedule extra time with you to get it completed on time.

Time Frame

- 1–2 weeks—Students are given the menu as the unit is started and the guidelines and point expectations on the top of the menu are discussed. Usually, students are expected to complete 100 points. Because this menu covers one topic in depth, the teacher will go over all of the options for the topic being covered and have students place check marks in the boxes next to the activities they are most interested in completing. As instruction continues, the activities are completed by students and submitted for grading.
- 1–2 days—The teacher chooses an activity from an objective to use with the entire class during the lesson time.

Suggested Forms

- All-purpose rubric
- Student-taught lesson rubric

Name:_____

Whole Numbers

Look through the following choices and decide how you want to make your game add to 100 points. Singles are worth 10 points, Doubles are worth 30 points, Triples are worth 50 points, and Homeruns are worth 100 points. Choose any combination you want! Place a check mark next to each choice you are going to complete. Make sure that your points equal 100!

Singles—10 Points Each
❑ Create a set of concentration cards for appropriate multiplication and division facts.

❑ Count the number of students in your class, and develop six word problems involving the number of students. Submit the problems and the solutions showing all the work.

❑ Design an instructional poster that shows the steps for completing complex addition, subtraction, multiplication, and division problems.

❑ Create a mathematical crossword puzzle in which the clues are the problems.

❑ Create a set of four trading cards: one each for multiplication, division, addition, and subtraction.

Doubles—30 Points Each
❑ Create a brochure about how mathematics is used in our everyday lives.

❑ Write a poem or jingle that shares the steps to solve a math problem using two-digit numbers.

❑ Create a cube with a different word problem on each side.

❑ Complete two Venn diagrams. One will compare and contrast addition and multiplication, and the other will compare and contrast subtraction and division.

❑ Make a board game to reinforce multiplication and division problem-solving skills.

❑ Design a book cover for a book about using multiplication in our everyday lives.

Triples—50 Points Each

❑ You have been given the task to create a shopping list that would supply enough food to feed your family for a week. Using the advertisements from the local grocery stores, develop your plan. You should plan on spending no more than $35 per person in your family. Make a report that shares the specific costs of your plan.

❑ Write a 1–2 page story using numbers, and then write 5 word problems using information presented in the story. Your problems should be creative and complex!

❑ Develop a lesson for your classmates that teaches them how to solve word problems with complex numbers and operations.

Homeruns—100 Points Each

❑ Create your own Mr. or Ms. Math Video in which you teach viewers about adding, subtracting, multiplying, and dividing. Your video should present basic problems, as well as word problems. It should also include at least three commercials for math-based products. Be creative and have fun!

I Chose:

_____ Singles (10 points each)

_____ Doubles (30 points each)

_____ Triples (50 points each)

_____ Homerun (100 points)

© Prufrock Press Inc. • *Differentiating Instruction With Menus: Math • Grades 3–5*
Permission is granted to photocopy or reproduce this page for single classroom use only.

Whole Numbers Cube

Complete the cube for whole numbers. Use this pattern or create your own cube. Each side of the cube should include a different word problem using whole numbers.

CHAPTER 6

Fractions

Basic Fractions

Tic-Tac-Toe Menu

Objectives Covered Through This Menu and These Activities
- Students will be able to name fractions.
- Students will be able to place fractions in order.
- Students will be able to show equivalent fractions.

Materials Needed by Students for Completion
- Graph paper or Internet access (for crossword puzzle)
- Materials for student-created manipulatives
- Video camera (for how-to video and commercial)
- Materials for board games (for folders, colored cards, etc.)
- Blank index cards (for concentration game)
- Cube template
- Recipe books

Time Frame
- 2 weeks—Students are given the menu as the unit is started. As the teacher presents lessons throughout the week, he or she refers back to the options associated with that content. The teacher will go over all of the options for that content and have students place check marks in the boxes that represent the activities they are most interested in completing. As teaching continues throughout the 2 weeks, the activities chosen and completed should make a column or a row. When students make this pattern, they have completed one activity from each content area: naming fractions, ordering fractions, and equivalent fractions.
- 1 week—At the start of the unit, the teacher chooses the three activities he or she feels are most valuable for the students. Stations can be set up in the classroom. These three activities are available for student choice throughout the week, as regular instruction takes place.
- 1–2 days—The teacher chooses an activity from the menu to use with the entire class.

Suggested Forms
- All-purpose rubric
- Proposal form for projects

Name:_____

Basic Fractions

☐ *Naming Fractions* Using one of your favorite recipes, convert all of the information (including the ingredient list) into a picture only recipe. You cannot use any words.	☐ *Ordering Fractions* Develop a set of manipulatives that you can use to show or teach ordering fractions.	☐ *Equivalent Fractions* Create a commercial that advertises a special item for sale. It should use equivalent fractions to try and trick the buyer into paying more for the same amount of product.
☐ *Equivalent Fractions* Create a product cube for a fraction of your choice. Each side should have a different equivalent fraction for the fraction you chose.	☐ ***Free Choice*** (Fill out your proposal form before beginning the free choice!)	☐ *Ordering Fractions* Create a game that tests your classmates' knowledge of putting fractions in order from greatest to least or least to greatest.
☐ *Ordering Fractions* Make a how-to video that would teach other students your age how to put fractions in order from least to greatest. Create a unique host for your how-to video.	☐ *Equivalent Fractions* Create a set of concentration cards for matching equivalent fractions. You can use pictures, words, or symbols.	☐ *Naming Fractions* Create a naming fractions crossword puzzle.

Check the boxes you plan to complete. They should form a tic-tac-toe across or down.
All products are due by: _____.

© Prufrock Press Inc. • *Differentiating Instruction With Menus: Math • Grades 3–5*
Permission is granted to photocopy or reproduce this page for single classroom use only.

Basic Fractions Cube

Complete the cube for a fraction of your choice. Use this pattern or create your own cube. Each side should have a different equivalent fraction for the fraction you chose.

© Prufrock Press Inc. • *Differentiating Instruction With Menus: Math* • *Grades 3–5*
Permission is granted to photocopy or reproduce this page for single classroom use only.

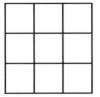

Adding and Subtracting Fractions

Tic-Tac-Toe Menu

Objectives Covered Through This Menu and These Activities
- Students will be able to add and subtract fractions.
- Students will be able to apply the addition and subtraction of fractions to real-world situations.

Materials Needed by Students for Completion
- Poster board or large white paper
- Materials for board games (file folders, colored cards, etc.)
- Materials for student created lessons (fraction manipulatives, etc.)
- Magazines
- Cube template
- Meter sticks (for measuring dimensions of the classroom)

Special Notes on the Use of This Menu
Be sure you have enough meter sticks for the classroom measurement activity. Students really like being able to apply their knowledge to real-world situations and having students measure the classroom for a new border is a lot of fun, but it can be distracting if class time is not planned for activity work. Students do not need to measure the top of the room (although they think they do)—they can just as easily measure around the bottom. Students can have additional fun by looking at wallpaper books obtained from home stores to propose ideas and even calculate costs for the border.

Time Frame
- 2 weeks—Students are given the menu as the unit is started. As the teacher presents lessons throughout the week, he or she refers back to the options associated with that content. The teacher will go over all of the options for that content and have students place check marks in the boxes that represent the activities they are most interested in completing. As teaching continues throughout the 2 weeks, the activities chosen and completed should make a column or a row.
- 1 week—At the start of the unit, the teacher chooses the three activities he or she feels are most valuable for the students. Stations can be set up in the classroom. These three activities are available for student choice throughout the week, as regular instruction takes place.

- 1–2 days—The teacher chooses an activity from the menu to use with the entire class.

Suggested Forms

- All-purpose rubric
- Student-taught lesson rubric
- Proposal form for projects

Name:_____

Adding and Subtracting Fractions

☐ *Make a Map* Create a map of your playground using a scale of every 3 feet equaling ¾ of an inch. Present your map on a poster.	☐ *You Create the Problem!* Create a cube with six word problems using fractions. Include three addition and three subtraction problems.	☐ *You Sing It!* Create a song or rap that tells the steps to follow when adding or subtracting fractions.
☐ *You Design it!* Design a worksheet where you show how to add and subtract fractions. Include some practice problems.	☐ **Free Choice** (Fill out your proposal form before beginning the free choice!)	☐ *You Play it!* Make a board game that tests your classmates' knowledge of adding and subtracting fractions.
☐ *Create a Collage* Using pictures from magazines, design four fraction word problems on a poster. Use the pictures to show how to complete each problem.	☐ *You Teach It!* Create a lesson for the class that teaches the addition and subtraction of fractions. Use manipulatives and allow your classmates to practice their skills!	☐ *A New Border* Your teacher wants to put a new border around the classroom. He or she will need accurate measurements, down the closest ⅛ of an inch. Measure your classroom and record the exact amount of border your teacher would need.

Check the boxes you plan to complete. They should form a tic-tac-toe across or down. All products are due by: _____.

Word Problem Cube

Complete the cube for adding and subtracting fractions. Use this pattern or create your own cube. Each side of the cube will include a word problem using fractions. Include three addition and three subtraction problems.

© Prufrock Press Inc. • *Differentiating Instruction With Menus: Math • Grades 3–5*
Permission is granted to photocopy or reproduce this page for single classroom use only.

Multiplying and Dividing Fractions

List Menu

Objectives Covered Through This Menu and These Activities

- Students will be able to multiply and divide fractions.
- Students will be able to show examples of fractions in their daily lives.
- Students will be able to solve problems using fractions.

Materials Needed by Students for Completion

- Graph paper or Internet access (for crossword puzzle)
- Magazines (for collage)
- Recipe books
- Microsoft PowerPoint or other slideshow software
- Blank index cards (for concentration card game)

Time Frame

- 1–2 weeks—Students are given the menu as the unit is started and the guidelines and point expectations on the menu are discussed. Because this menu covers one topic in depth, the teacher will go over all the options for the topic being covered and have students place check marks in the boxes next to the activities they are most interested in completing. As instruction continues, the activities are completed by students and submitted for grading.
- 1–2 days—The teacher chooses an activity from an objective to use with the entire class during that lesson time.

Suggested Forms

- All-purpose rubric
- Proposal form for point-based projects

Name:_____

Multiplying and Dividing Fractions

Guidelines:

1. You may complete as many of the activities as you would like listed within the time period given.
2. You may choose any combination of activities.
3. Your goal is 100 points. You may earn up to _____ points extra credit.
4. You may be as creative as you like within the guidelines listed below.
5. You must show your plan to your teacher by _____.
6. Activities may be turned in at any time during the working time period. They will be graded and recorded on this sheet as you continue to work, so keep it safe!

Plan to Do	Activity to Complete	Point Value	Date Completed	Points Earned
	Choose your favorite recipe. Your friends have decided to prepare it for a party 50 people. Create a grocery list for the total amount of items they will need to buy.	25		
	Make an "Understanding Fractions" brochure that explains how to add, subtract, multiply, and divide fractions. Include examples.	15		
	Create a cartoon in which the main character, One Half, has to divide itself. Be creative about why this has to happen and how it takes place.	25		
	Create a number crossword puzzle for different fraction problems.	20		
	Design a PowerPoint presentation that teaches students how to multiply fractions. Include various examples.	20		
	Create a collage that shows various examples of using fractions in our daily lives.	15		
	Create a set of concentration cards that match multiplication and division problems with their answers.	15		
	Write a children's story about a fraction that has to keep multiplying.	25		
	Create an advertisement for a new machine that will complete a student's fraction problems for them. Explain how the machine works.	20		
	Your school librarian has asked your class for some help on the purchase of some new bookcases with two shelves each. She has 300 new books she needs to shelve. One half of the books are half an inch thick. One third of them are one fourth of an inch thick, and the rest are three fourths of an inch thick. Her shelves are 30 inches long. How many bookcases should she buy? Show your work.	30		
	Free choice: Must be outlined on a proposal form and approved before beginning work.			
	Total number of points you are planning to earn.		**Total points earned:**	

I am planning to complete _____ activities that could earn up to a total of _____ points.

Teacher's initials _____ Student's signature _____

© Prufrock Press Inc. • *Differentiating Instruction With Menus: Math • Grades 3–5*
Permission is granted to photocopy or reproduce this page for single classroom use only.

CHAPTER 7

Probability
and Statistics

Using Graphs

2-5-8 Menu

Objectives Covered Through This Menu and These Activities

*   Students will be able to distinguish between different types of graphs.
*   Students will be able to read graphs and interpret the data presented.
*   Students will be able to create graphs from data.

Materials Needed by Students for Completion

*   Poster board or large white paper
*   Materials for student-created experiments
*   Newspapers
*   Button bucket (a large container of different types and sizes of buttons)
*   Circle graph activity (see Situation Graph)

Time Frame

*   1–2 weeks—Students are given the menu as the unit is started, and the teacher discusses all of the product options on the menu. As the different options are discussed, students will choose products that add to a total of 10 points. As the lessons progress through the week, the teacher and the students should refer back to the options associated with the content being taught.
*   1–2 days—The teacher chooses an activity from the menu to use with the entire class.

Suggested Forms

*   All-purpose rubric
*   Proposal form for point-based projects

Using Graphs

Directions: Choose two activities from the menu below. The activities must total 10 points. Place a check mark in each box to show which activities you will complete. All activities must be completed by

_____.

---

2 Points

❒ Using a newspaper, locate three different graphs. Write a brief summary of what each graph is showing.

❒ Create a poster that shows all of the different types of graphs. Include a real-life example of each graph, tell the benefits of the graph, and explain when it should be used to show data.

---

5 Points

❒ Design a survey to obtain your classmates' answers to a popular question. Present your information on a poster using a circle graph.

❒ Using the button bucket, create a graph that represents its contents.

❒ Prepare a data source for a line graph and complete the line graph.

❒ Given the circle graph (Situation Graph, p. 74), create a situation that could match the data.

---

8 Points

❒ Design your own experiment or survey. Write the steps for conducting your task. Record your information in a data table, and create a graph to show your results. You may use Microsoft Excel to create your graph.

❒ Free choice—Prepare a proposal form and submit it to your teacher for approval.

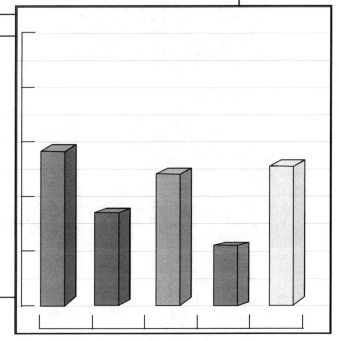

Situation Graph

Examine the circle graph below and develop a situation that could match this graph. Be creative!

© Prufrock Press Inc. • *Differentiating Instruction With Menus: Math* • *Grades 3–5*
Permission is granted to photocopy or reproduce this page for single classroom use only.

Mean, Median, and Mode

2-5-8 Menu

Objectives Covered Through This Menu and These Activities
- Students will be able to calculate the mean, median, and mode of data.
- Students will understand the real-world applications of mean, median, and mode.

Materials Needed by Students for Completion
- Microsoft PowerPoint or other slideshow software
- Sports section of the newspaper
- Dice
- Materials for student-designed lessons

Time Frame
- 1–2 weeks—Students are given the menu as the unit is started, and the teacher discusses all of the product options on the menu. As the different options are discussed, students will choose products that add to a total of 10 points. As the lessons progress through the week, the teacher and the students should refer back to the options associated with the content being taught.
- 1–2 days—The teacher chooses an activity from the menu to use with the entire class.

Suggested Forms
- All-purpose rubric
- Student-taught lesson rubric
- Proposal form for point-based projects

Mean, Median, and Mode

Directions: Choose two activities from the menu below. The activities must total 10 points. Place a check mark in each box to show which activities you will complete. All activities must be completed by _____.

2 Points

❐ Create a PowerPoint presentation that shows how to find the mean, median, and mode of data. Include at least one real-world example.

❐ Make a brochure that explains mean, median, and mode. It should explain how to find each and what each tells about the data.

5 Points

❐ Using the sports section of the newspaper, research the statistics of at least 20 players in one sport. After gathering the data, record the mean, median, and mode for the players. Explain what each number means to the sport.

❐ Are dice really random? Record a hypothesis about what patterns will happen if you roll a set of dice 100 times. Roll the dice and record your data. Find the mean, median, and mode for your data.

❐ Create a questionnaire to gather data from three questions. Have at least 10 people complete your questionnaire. Present the mean, mode, and median of your data.

❐ Are you the mean, mode, or median in your classroom? Choose one physical aspect of your classmates (for example, height, diameter of head, length of hands, etc.) and record the measurements for your classmates. Then, show the mean, median, and mode of your gathered information.

8 Points

❐ Design a class lesson in which the entire class gathers data and calculates the mean, median, and mode of the data.

❐ Free choice—Prepare a proposal form and submit to your teacher for approval.

© Prufrock Press Inc. • *Differentiating Instruction With Menus: Math • Grades 3–5*
Permission is granted to photocopy or reproduce this page for single classroom use only.

CHAPTER 8

Geometry

Circles

2-5-8 Menu

Objectives Covered Through This Menu and These Activities

- Students will be able to calculate the radius, diameter, and circumference of a circle.
- Students will understand the relationship between the measurements of radius and circumference.
- Students will be able to use properties of a circle to solve real-world problems.

Materials Needed by Students for Completion

- Poster board or large white paper
- Materials for student-created measuring activity (such as flexible measuring tape)
- Magazines (for collage)
- Video camera (for news report)
- Microsoft PowerPoint or other slideshow software

Time Frame

- 1–2 weeks—Students are given the menu as the unit is started, and the teacher discusses all of the product options on the menu. As the different options are discussed, students will choose products that add to a total of 10 points. As the lessons progress through the week, the teacher and the students should refer back to the options associated with the content being taught.
- 1–2 days—The teacher chooses an activity from the menu to use with the entire class.

Suggested Forms

- All-purpose rubric
- Proposal form for point-based projects

Name:_____

Circles

Directions: Choose two activities from the menu below. The activities must total 10 points. Place a check mark in each box to show which activities you will complete. All activities must be completed by _____.

2 Points

❏ Create a worksheet for your classmates about calculating the radius, diameter, and circumference of a circle.

❏ Create a collage of circular objects. Record the radius, diameter, and circumference for each object.

5 Points

❏ Create a song or rap to help you remember the different parts of a circle.

❏ Your teacher would like to buy the largest circular rug she can use to cover your classroom floor. Circular rugs are sold by diameter. Make a poster to propose to your teacher the size of rug he or she should purchase. Include a drawing of the pattern and colors you think would be best.

❏ Circles have a lot of practical uses in science. Create a PowerPoint presentation that shows at least five examples of how circles and the measures of their radii (plural of radius) are used in science.

❏ Free choice—Prepare a proposal form and submit to your teacher for approval.

8 Points

❏ There is a special relationship between the diameter and the circumference of a circle. Design a measuring activity that allows you to figure out this relationship. You should test at least 10 objects to confirm your results.

❏ There has been a crime committed! Create a news report in which the circumference of a circle helped solve the crime.

Lines and Congruency

2-5-8 Menu

Objective Covered Through This Menu and These Activities

- Students will be able to identify perpendicular and parallel lines and their properties in real-world situations.

Materials Needed by Students for Completion

- Graph paper or Internet access (for crossword puzzle)
- Materials for student-created artwork (colored pencils, large paper, etc.)
- Magazines (pictures of buildings)
- Coat hangers (for mobile)
- Index cards (for mobile)
- String (for mobile)
- Information on M. C. Escher

Time Frame

- 1–2 weeks— Students are given the menu as the unit is started, and the teacher discusses all of the product options on the menu. As the different options are discussed, students will choose products that add to a total of 10 points. As the lessons progress through the week, the teacher and the students should refer back to the options associated with the content being taught.
- 1–2 days—The teacher chooses an activity from the menu to use with the entire class.

Suggested Forms

- All-purpose rubric
- Proposal form for point-based projects

Name:_____

Lines and Congruency

Directions: Choose two activities from the menu below. The activities must total 10 points. Place a check mark in each box to show which activities you will complete. All activities must be completed by _____.

2 Points

❐ Create a worksheet to quiz your classmates about the difference between *parallel* and *perpendicular,* as well as how to tell if two figures are congruent.

❐ Make a mobile that shows examples of parallel and perpendicular lines.

5 Points

❐ Collect 10 photos from magazines that show parallel and perpendicular lines. Create a collage or folder with these photos. Mark each set of parallel or perpendicular lines.

❐ When designing a building, using congruent pieces is sometimes very important. Collect pictures of buildings from magazines that were built using congruent or noncongruent parts. Label each part and tell how they impacted the structure.

❐ Make a crossword puzzle with parallel and perpendicular items as the clues.

❐ Free choice—Prepare a proposal form and submit to your teacher for approval.

8 Points

❐ Write a story that details the adventures of the archenemies: Parallel Boy and Perpendicular Girl.

❐ M. C. Escher was an artist who had many interesting styles. One of his techniques used congruent figures to create new and different patterns. Research this type of artwork and create a sample of your own based on his method.

Geometry–Shapes

Tic-Tac-Toe Menu

Objectives Covered Through This Menu and These Activities

- Students will be able to identify lines of symmetry in everyday objects.
- Students will be able to name and identify various geometric figures.
- Students will be able to identify the number of vertices, faces, and edges on geometric figures.
- Students will be able to measure different geometric shapes.

Materials Needed by Students for Completion

- Poster board or large white paper
- Materials for board games (folders, colored cards, etc.)
- Magazines (symmetry pictures)
- Blank index cards (for trading cards)
- Shoe boxes (for dioramas)
- Materials for bedroom models
- Cube template

Time Frame

- 2 weeks—Students are given the menu as the unit is started. As the teacher presents lessons throughout the week, students refer back to the options associated with that content. The teacher will go over all of the options for that content and have students place check marks in the boxes that represent the activities they are most interested in completing. As teaching continues throughout the 2 weeks, the activities chosen and completed should make a column or a row. When students make this pattern, they have completed one activity from each content area: lines of symmetry, naming and describing geometric shapes and solids, and measuring geometric shapes and solids.
- 1 week—At the start of the unit, the teacher chooses the three activities he or she feels are most valuable for the students. Stations can be set up in the classroom. These three activities are available for student choice throughout the week, as regular instruction takes place.
- 1–2 days—The teacher chooses an activity from the menu to use with the entire class.

Suggested Forms

- All-purpose rubric
- Proposal form for projects
- $1 contract (diorama, puppet)

Name:_____

Geometry—Shapes

☐ *Symmetry*	☐ *Measuring Shapes*	☐ *Naming and Describing*
Using a magazine, cut out 10 pictures of objects that have exactly one line of symmetry. Present your pictures on a poster with the line of symmetry carefully marked on each.	Create a brochure that explains how to measure the perimeter, area, and volume of different objects.	Create a model or diorama of your bedroom using examples of the geometric shapes. Create a key that tells the shapes that create each object, as well as the number of vertices, faces, and edges for each.
☐ *Naming and Describing* Create a set of trading cards for all of the geometric shapes and solids. Include the number of vertices, faces, and edges for each.	☐ **Free Choice** (Fill out your proposal form before beginning the free choice!)	☐ *Measuring Shapes* Find household examples of eight different shapes and solids. Measure each one and in a chart, record its perimeter, area, and volume.
☐ *Measuring Shapes* Create a board game in which players will need to calculate and measure the perimeter, area, and volume of objects in order to play.	☐ *Naming and Describing* Complete a cube with one geometric shape or solid on each side. Give a real-world example of each shape, as well as the number of vertices, faces, and edges for each.	☐ *Symmetry* Create a drawing of a nature scene in which each object in your drawing has exactly two lines of symmetry. Be creative in your drawing!

Check the boxes you plan to complete. They should form a tic-tac-toe across or down. All products are due by: _____.

Geometry Shapes Cube

Complete the cube for geometric shapes. Use this pattern or create your own cube. Place one geometric shape or solid on each side along with a real-world example of the shape, and the number of vertices, faces, and edges for the shape.

© Prufrock Press Inc. • *Differentiating Instruction With Menus: Math • Grades 3–5*
Permission is granted to photocopy or reproduce this page for single classroom use only.

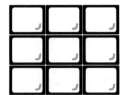

Geometry
Game Show Menu

Objectives Covered Through This Menu and These Activities

- Students will be able to calculate area, perimeter, and volume of various geometric shapes.
- Students will be able to identify geometric shapes and solids.
- Students will be able to count vertices, edges, and faces of geometric solids.

Materials Needed by Students for Completion

- Poster board or large white paper
- Materials for board games (file folders, colored cards, etc.)
- Materials for student-created volume activities
- Materials for measuring shapes (rulers, measuring tapes, etc.)
- Video camera (for artistic video)
- Coat hangers (for mobile)
- Index cards (for mobile)
- String (for mobile)
- Microsoft PowerPoint or other slideshow software
- Materials for modern art project
- Scrapbooking materials

Special Notes on the Use of This Menu

This menu has students measure their school library for carpet. Librarians like to be informed about these kinds of matters, and students sometimes get caught up with counting each small detail along the floor. Evaluate the perimeter of the library and give helpful hints to students about estimating when appropriate.

Time Frame

- 2–3 weeks—Students are given the menu as the unit is started and the guidelines and point expectations on the menu are discussed. As lessons are taught throughout the unit, students and the teacher can refer back to the options associated with that topic. The teacher will go over all of the options for the topic being covered and have students place check marks in the boxes next to the activities they are most interested in completing. As teaching continues throughout the

2–3 weeks, the activities are discussed, chosen, and submitted for grading.

- 1 week—At the beginning of the unit, the teacher chooses an activity from each area that he or she feels would be most valuable for the students. Stations can be set up in the classroom. These activities are available for student choice throughout the week, as regular instruction takes place.
- 1–2 days—The teacher chooses an activity from an objective to use with the entire class during that lesson time.

Suggested Forms

- All-purpose rubric
- Student-taught lesson rubric
- Proposal form for point-based projects
- $1 contract (diorama, puppet)

Guidelines for Geometry Game Show Menu

- You must choose at least one activity from each topic area.
- You may not do more than two activities in any one topic area for credit. (You are, of course, welcome to do more than two for your own investigation.)
- Grading will be ongoing, so turn in products as you complete them.
- All free-choice proposals must be turned in and approved *prior* to working on that free choice.
- You must earn 120 points for a 100%. You may earn extra credit up to _____ points.
- You must show your teacher your plan for completion by: _____.

Geometry

	Shapes	Geometric Solids	Vertices, Edges, and Faces	Area	Perimeter	Volume	Points for Each Level
	☐ Create a mobile that shows all of the different shapes and characteristics of each. (10 pts.)	☐ Find two real-world examples in your home for each geometric solid. Bring your examples to share. (15 pts.)	☐ Create a PowerPoint presentation that shows the vertices, edges, and faces of everyday objects. (15 pts.)	☐ Create a poster that shows how to find the area of at least three different shapes. (10 pts.)	☐ Choose three items from home and measure their perimeter. Present the objects and your data to the class. (15 pts.)	☐ Create a brochure that shows examples of the different solids and explains how to calculate the volume of each. (10 pts.)	**10–15 Points**
	☐ Create a board game based on geometric shares and their properties. (20 pts.)	☐ Create a scrapbook for one of the geometric solids. It should show its impact on our daily lives. (25 pts.)	☐ Create a song about the number of vertices, edges, and faces on geometric solids. (20 pts.)	☐ Complete a Venn diagram to compare area and perimeter. (20 pts.)	☐ Create an advertisement for a product where its perimeter is its main selling point. (25 pts.)	☐ Create an activity that helps your classmates practice measuring volume. (25 pts.)	**20–25 Points**
	☐ Write an original story about a shape and its adventures. The special properties of the shape should help in its story. (30 pts.)	☐ Using at least five different solid shapes, create your own piece of modern art. Include a key that describes the different solids used. (30 pts.)	☐ Many artists use the lines of geometric forms in their work. Make an artistic video about vertices, edges, and faces that we see every day. (30 pts.)	☐ You have been given the task of recarpeting your school's library. Develop a plan for how to accomplish this task. After measuring the library, make a proposal for the amount of carpet needed and a reasonable cost. (30 pts.)	☐ Your school is thinking of putting a new fence all the way around your building. Develop a plan for how to calculate the amount of fencing needed. Complete your plan. (30 pts.)	☐ As a practical joke, you have decided to fill your classroom with popped popcorn. Develop your calculation method to determine how much can fit. After taking some measurements, propose the amount of popped popcorn it would take. (30 pts.)	**30 Points**
	Free Choice (prior approval) (25–50 pts.)	**Free Choice** (prior approval) (25–50 pts.)	**Free Choice** (prior approval) (25–50 pts.)	**Free Choice** (prior approval) (25–50 pts.)	**Free Choice** (prior approval) (25–50 pts.)	**Free Choice** (prior approval) (25–50 pts.)	**25–50 Points**
	Total:	Total:	Total:	Total:	Total:	Total:	**Total Grade:**

© Prufrock Press Inc. • *Differentiating Instruction With Menus: Math • Grades 3–5*
Permission is granted to photocopy or reproduce this page for single classroom use only.

Chapter 9

Measurement

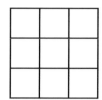

Measuring Capacity
Tic-Tac-Toe Menu

Objectives Covered Through This Menu and These Activities

- Students will be able to use milliliters, liters, cups, pints, and gallons to measure capacity.
- Students will be able to estimate capacity using both standard and metric units.
- Students will be able to solve real-world problems in both standard and metric units.

Materials Needed by Students for Completion

- Poster board or large white paper
- Newspapers
- Metric measuring lab
- Gallon person handout (see Gallon Person)
- Materials for student-created experiments

Special Notes on the Use of This Menu

This menu allows students to create an experiment for measuring capacity. This works best when students are given the equipment before beginning their designed experiment.

Time Frame

- 2 weeks—Students are given the menu as the unit is started. As the teacher presents lessons throughout the week, students refer back to the options associated with that content. The teacher will go over all of the options for that content and have students place check marks in the boxes that represent the activities they are most interested in completing. As teaching continues throughout the 2 weeks, the activities chosen and completed should make a column or a row. When students make this pattern, they have completed one activity from each content area: metric units for capacity, standard units of capacity, and capacity in the real world.
- 1 week—At the start of the unit, the teacher chooses the three activities he or she feels are most valuable for the students. Stations can be set up in the classroom. These three activities are available for student choice throughout the week, as regular instruction takes place.

- 1–2 days—The teacher chooses an activity from the menu to use with the entire class.

Suggested Forms

- All-purpose rubric
- Student-taught lesson rubric
- Proposal form for projects

Measuring Capacity

☐ *Capacity in Our World* Create a flipbook for each unit of capacity: milliliters, liters, cups, pints, gallons, and quarts. On each page, create a math problem that involves that unit. The problem should be realistic.	☐ *Metric Units* All household items that hold liquids need to be marked in both metric and standard units. Develop a system to test the accuracy of these recorded measurements. Test four household items and present your data in a table.	☐ *Standard Units* Create a poster showing the gallon person. Create each part of the body out of items that would be measured in that unit.
☐ *Standard Units* Create a capacity collection. Collect two household items that are measured in each unit: cups, pints, quarts, and gallons. This will give you a total of eight items to bring to class.	☐ **Free Choice** (Fill out your proposal form before beginning the free choice!)	☐ *Metric Units* Design an experiment in which your classmates would practice estimating and measuring in milliliters and liters.
☐ *Metric Units* Your neighbors are purchasing a new pool. Their backyard is quite large (20 yards wide and 30 yards deep). Unfortunately, the pool dealer will only deal in liter-sized pools. Research pool sizes and decide on the largest amount of liters their pool could hold based on the size of their backyard.	☐ *Standard Units* Create an activity in which your classmates would practice estimating and measuring cups, pints, quarts, and gallons.	☐ *Capacity in Our World* Search through a newspaper to find articles or advertisements that use units of capacity. Create a poster collage that shows all of your examples.

Check the boxes you plan to complete. They should form a tic-tac-toe across or down. All products are due by: _____.

© Prufrock Press Inc. • *Differentiating Instruction With Menus: Math • Grades 3–5*
 Permission is granted to photocopy or reproduce this page for single classroom use only.

Name:_____

Gallon Person

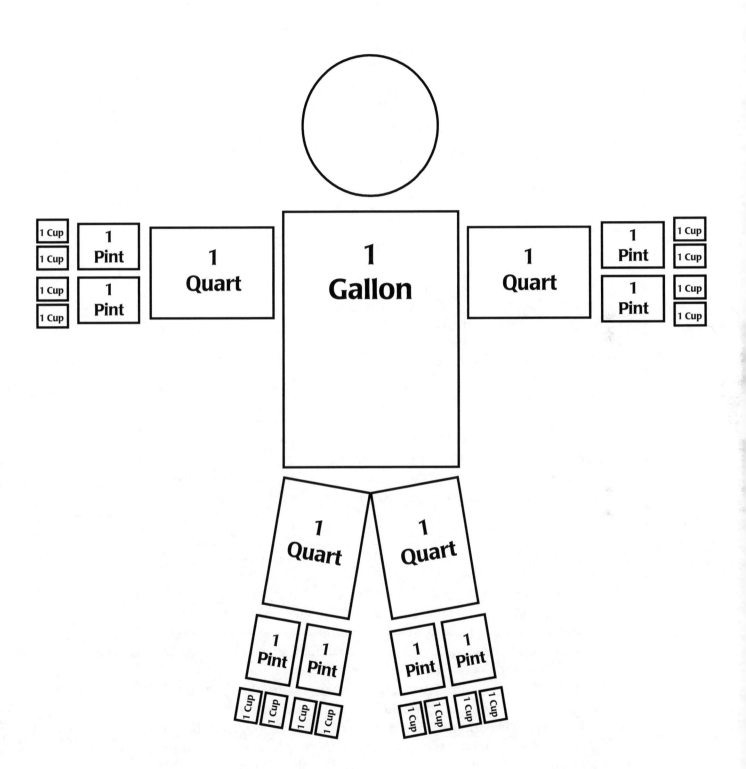

Time

Tic-Tac-Toe Menu

Objectives Covered Through This Menu and These Activities

- Students will be able to explain the importance of telling time.
- Students will be able to solve real-world problems using time and schedules.

Materials Needed by Students for Completion

- Poster board or large white paper
- Magazines (collage)
- Microsoft PowerPoint or other slideshow software
- Blank index cards (concentration card game)
- Page from newspaper with daily movie times
- Access to the Internet and airline Web sites
- School schedule activity (see Create Your Own School Schedule)

Special Notes on the Use of This Menu

This menu allows the students to create their own race around the world. This works best when students have access to world maps and the different airline Web sites. The students can choose the date for their "race" and see what flights can be found. This is a time-intensive activity because there are so many options available.

Time Frame

- 2 weeks—Students are given the menu as the unit is started. As the teacher presents lessons throughout the week, students refer back to the options associated with that content. The teacher will go over all of the options for that content and have students place check marks in the boxes that represent the activities they are most interested in completing. As teaching continues throughout the 2 weeks, the activities chosen and completed should make a column or a row.
- 1 week—At the start of the unit, the teacher chooses the three activities he or she feels are most valuable for the students. Stations can be set up in the classroom. These three activities are available for student choice throughout the week, as regular instruction takes place.
- 1–2 days—The teacher chooses an activity from the menu to use with the entire class.

Suggested Forms

- All-purpose rubric
- Proposal form for projects

Name: _____

Time

☐ **It Is All About Time!** Create a poster that explains how to read both a digital and an analog clock.	☐ **Time Zones** There are many time zones around the world (even in the United States). Prepare a PowerPoint presentation that describes the reason for time zones and why their locations are defined as they are.	☐ **Your Own Schedule** Thinking about all of the components that go into creating a schedule, complete the Create Your Own School Schedule activity.
☐ **Around the World?** You are participating in a race around the world, visiting at least six major cities of your choice. Using the Internet to find the schedules of major airlines, prepare an itinerary that shows the fastest route to visit all six cities.	☐ **Free Choice** (Fill out your proposal form before beginning the free choice!)	☐ **Digital vs. Analog Clocks** A group of students would like our state to change its policy on learning how to tell time. They don't think that students need to learn anything except how to read a digital clock. Do you agree? Why or why not? Prepare a pamphlet that shows your point of view.
☐ **Is Time Important?** Make a collage that shows the importance of telling time. Include practical and creative examples.	☐ **Movie Marathon** A movie theater is holding a daylong movie marathon for just $10. Analyze current movie times and create a schedule that allows you to see as many movies as possible within the day. You cannot leave one movie for another.	☐ **Do You Have the Time?** Create a concentration game for clocks and the time they tell.

Check the boxes you plan to complete. They should form a tic-tac-toe across or down. All products are due by: _____.

Name:_____

Create Your Own School Schedule

You have been presented with the task to create a workable schedule for the students in your grade level. Here is what you will need to consider:

- Students must spend at least 45 minutes a day on each subject area (math, science, language arts, and social studies).
- Students must have at least 30 minutes for lunch.
- Students must have at least 45 minutes each day for elective time (for example, physical education, music, library, etc.).
- Your school day should start and finish at the same times it does now.

Using these guidelines, design the perfect weekly schedule for your classmates. You may be creative in rotating the elective classes each day, and allowing recess or extra time during lunches as time allows. Make your presentation of your schedule on a large poster board. Include the advantages and disadvantages for your schedule.

Use the chart below to brainstorm your ideas.

Times	Monday	Tuesday	Wednesday	Thursday	Friday

What are the advantages and disadvantages to your plan?

© Prufrock Press Inc. • *Differentiating Instruction With Menus: Math • Grades 3–5*
Permission is granted to photocopy or reproduce this page for single classroom use only.

Measuring Length

2-5-8 Menu

Objectives Covered Through This Menu and These Activities

- Students will be able to use centimeters, meters, inches, feet, and yards to measure length.
- Students will be able to estimate length using both standard and metric units.
- Students will be able to solve real-world problems in both standard and metric units.

Materials Needed by Students for Completion

- Poster board or large white paper
- Materials for Guess the Measure game (classroom objects)
- Materials for student-created models
- Video camera (for educational videos)
- Tools for measuring (meter sticks, rulers)
- Coat hangers (for mobile)
- Index cards (for mobile)
- String (for mobile)
- Microsoft PowerPoint or other slideshow software
- Newspapers

Time Frame

- 1–2 weeks—Students are given the menu as the unit is started, and the teacher discusses all of the product options on the menu. As the different options are discussed, students will choose products that add to a total of 10 points. As the lessons progress through the week, the teacher and the students should refer back to the options associated with the content being taught.
- 1–2 days—The teacher chooses an activity from the menu to use with the entire class.

Suggested Forms

- All-purpose rubric
- Proposal form for point-based projects

Name:_____

Measuring Length

Directions: Choose two activities from the menu below. The activities must total 10 points. Place a check mark in each box to show which activities you will complete. All activities must be completed by _____.

2 Points

❒ Create a mobile with the different units for measuring length, and an example of an object that would be best measured with each unit.

❒ Go through the newspaper to locate articles that give examples of length. Prepare a poster with at least eight examples.

5 Points

❒ Create a map of your school. (You may have to do some measuring!) Develop a scale for your map using appropriate units.

❒ Design a PowerPoint presentation that shows how to choose the proper units for measuring lengths. Include information on how to properly measure length.

❒ Create a "guess the measure" game. In this game, players will need to estimate and measure the length of target items. Be creative in the design of the game.

❒ Free choice—Prepare a proposal form and submit it to your teacher for approval.

8 Points

❒ Create your own educational video on estimating and measuring length.

❒ Choose a large item in your home that you could rebuild using wood. After measuring all of the parts you would need to re-create the item, write the re-creation instructions with exact measurements. Also include a total parts list with estimations for each item.

© Prufrock Press Inc. • *Differentiating Instruction With Menus: Math • Grades 3–5*
Permission is granted to photocopy or reproduce this page for single classroom use only.

Measuring Temperature

Tic-Tac-Toe Menu

Objectives Covered Through This Menu and These Activities

- Students will be able to use thermometers to measure temperature.
- Students will be able to estimate temperature.
- Students will be able to solve real-world problems using temperature.

Materials Needed by Students for Completion

- Poster board or large white paper
- Graph paper (for graphing temperature)
- Newspapers
- Measuring temperature activity (see Measuring Temperature)
- Cups (for measuring temperature activity)
- Graduated cylinder (for measuring temperature activity)
- Thermometers (for measuring temperature activity)
- Ice cubes (for measuring temperature activity)

Special Notes on the Use of This Menu

Although this menu does include an experiment, it involves relatively few supplies and can be set up as a station for the students. Students can either come to the station or take the station to their desk to complete this activity.

Time Frame

- 2 weeks—Students are given the menu as the unit is started. As the teacher presents lessons throughout the week, students refer back to the options associated with that content. The teacher will go over all of the options for that content and have students place check marks in the boxes that represent the activities they are most interested in completing. As teaching continues throughout the 2 weeks, the activities chosen and completed should make a column or a row. When students make this pattern, they have completed one activity from each content area: estimating temperature, using temperature, and measuring temperature.
- 1 week—At the start of the unit, the teacher chooses the three activities he or she feels are most valuable for the students. Stations can be set up in the classroom. These three activities are available for student choice throughout the week, as regular instruction takes place.

- 1–2 days—The teacher chooses an activity from the menu to use with the entire class.

Suggested Forms

- All-purpose rubric
- Proposal form for projects

Name:_____

Measuring Temperature

☐ *Estimating Temperature* Create a worksheet that asks students to estimate temperatures around them.	☐ *Measuring Temperature* Complete the measuring temperature activity.	☐ *Using Temperature* Cut out the national temperature chart in your newspaper for one week. Choose three cities in different parts of the United States. Create a graph to show how the temperature has changed throughout the week.
☐ *Using Temperature* Create a children's book about temperature. The book should tell readers about different temperatures and how they may affect their daily lives.	☐ **Free Choice** (Fill out your proposal form before beginning the free choice!)	☐ *Measuring Temperature* Design your own lesson on measuring temperature. It should be a lesson that can be done at school.
☐ *Measuring Temperature* Using the thermometer, measure the temperature of two different locations in your school for one week. Create a data table to record your information. Write a conclusion that shares your finding and explains any surprises.	☐ *Using Temperature* Certain household items have temperature restrictions for their use. They work best only during certain temperatures. Find eight examples of these items. Prepare a poster that shows the items and how temperature affects them.	☐ *Estimating Temperature* Create a pamphlet to help other students your age better estimate temperature. Include specific examples and a quiz to test their abilities.

Check the boxes you plan to complete. They should form a tic-tac-toe across or down.
All products are due by: _____.

Measuring Temperature

Materials: four cups, water, ice cubes, thermometer

Procedure:
1. Put 100ml of tap water into each cup.
2. Record the temperature of each cup. (They should be very close in temperature because they are from the same water source.)
3. Look at your data table and make some predictions about how you think ice cubes will change the temperature of the water. For each cup, fill in the temperature you think will result from the melting of the ice cubes.
4. In the first cup, place one ice cube.
5. In the second cup, place two ice cubes.
6. In the third cup, place three ice cubes.
7. In the fourth cup, place four ice cubes.
8. Allow the ice cubes to melt in each cup.
9. Measure the temperature in each cup and calculate how close your guesses were.
10. Empty your cups and clean up your area.

Data:

Cup	Temperature Without Ice	Your Prediction Temperature	Actual Temperature	Difference
1				
2				
3				
4				

Questions:
1. Using all of your information, how much temperature change will one ice cube make?

2. If you had to predict the temperature change for 10 ice cubes, what would you predict as the new temperature? Explain your reasoning.

© Prufrock Press Inc. • *Differentiating Instruction With Menus: Math • Grades 3–5*
Permission is granted to photocopy or reproduce this page for single classroom use only.

Measuring Weight

Tic-Tac-Toe Menu

Objectives Covered Through This Menu and These Activities
- Students will be able to measure weight in standard and metric units.
- Students will be able to estimate weight using both standard and metric units.
- Students will be able to solve real-world problems in both standard and metric units.

Materials Needed by Students for Completion
- Triple beam balances
- Bucket of items (various classroom items)
- Internet access for postage information (http://www.usps.com)

Time Frame
- 2 weeks—Students are given the menu as the unit is started. As the teacher presents lessons throughout the week, students refer back to the options associated with that content. The teacher will go over all of the options for that content and have students place check marks in the boxes that represent the activities they are most interested in completing. As teaching continues throughout the 2 weeks, the activities chosen and completed should make a column or a row.
- 1 week—At the start of the unit, the teacher chooses the three activities he or she feels are most valuable for the students. Stations can be set up in the classroom. These three activities are available for student choice throughout the week, as regular instruction takes place.
- 1–2 days—The teacher chooses an activity from the menu to use with the entire class.

Suggested Forms
- All-purpose rubric
- Proposal form for projects

Name:_____

Measuring Weight

☐ *Does It Carry Weight?* Elevators always have a weight limit for safety. If an elevator can only hold 2,000 pounds, how many of your math books could the elevator carry at one time?	☐ *How Much Is One?* Create a flipbook for one ounce, one pound, one gram, and one kilogram. Inside each flap, draw at least three items that are close to these measurements.	☐ *Worth Reading* You have decided that you want to share your favorite book with your pen pal who lives in a nearby state. The post office charges by weight, so weigh your book and determine how much it would cost to send it to your pen pal.
☐ *Are They All the Same?* Weight is often used in packaging, rather than counting items. How accurate is this method? Choose a product that is packaged based on weight in grams rather than a count of the items and devise a way to confirm the accuracy of this method.	☐ **Free Choice** (Fill out your proposal form before beginning the free choice!)	☐ *Make a Collection* Choose one unit of weight you would like to investigate. Collect household objects that show one unit of that mass (for example, objects that all weigh one pound). Bring your collection to school to share with your classmates.
☐ *Are You a Good Guesser?* Using the bucket of items provided by your teacher, predict the weight of each item. Create a data chart to record your predictions. Then weigh the items and record their actual weight. Include one column to record how close you were for each item.	☐ *Do You Know Your Weights?* Develop a strategy that would help you accurately guess an object's weight in grams and ounces. Record your method, all of your trials, and be ready to show your skill to your classmates.	☐ *Could You Board?* The Fly By Night Airline has decided to limit the weight of passenger luggage. They have decided that every passenger can only take 29 pounds of luggage with them on any trip. You plan to travel for 2 weeks, and your empty suitcase weighs 3 pounds. List the items you would take on your trip and the weight of each.

Check the boxes you plan to complete. They should form a tic-tac-toe across or down. All products are due by: _____.

© Prufrock Press Inc. • *Differentiating Instruction With Menus: Math • Grades 3–5*
Permission is granted to photocopy or reproduce this page for single classroom use only.

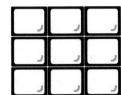

Measurement

Game Show Menu

Objectives Covered Through This Menu and These Activities

- Students will be able to estimate length, capacity, weight, and temperature in standard and metric units.
- Students will be able to measure length, capacity, weight, and temperature in standard and metric units.
- Students will be able to solve problems using length, capacity, weight, and temperature in standard and metric units.

Materials Needed by Students for Completion

- Materials for student-created models (for bridge model)
- Coat hangers (for mobile)
- Index cards (for mobile)
- String (for mobile)
- Gallon person handout (see Gallon Person, p. 93)
- Newspapers
- Materials for measurement (triple beam balances, tape measures, graduated cylinders, etc.)

Time Frame

- 2–3 weeks—Students are given the menu as the unit is started, and the guidelines and point expectations on the menu are discussed. As lessons are taught throughout the unit, the students and the teacher can refer back to the options associated with that topic. The teacher will go over all of the options for the topic being covered and have students place check marks in the boxes next to the activities they are most interested in completing. As teaching continues throughout 2–3 weeks, the activities are discussed, chosen, and submitted for grading.
- 1 week—At the beginning of the unit, the teacher chooses an activity from each area that he or she feels would be most valuable for the students. Stations can be set up in the classroom. These activities are available for student choice throughout the week, as regular instruction takes place.
- 1–2 days—The teacher chooses an activity from an objective to use with the entire class during that lesson time.

Suggested Forms

- All-purpose rubric
- Oral presentation rubric
- Student-taught lesson rubric
- Proposal form for point-based projects
- $1 contract (for diorama, puppet)

Guidelines for Measurement Game Show Menu

- You must choose at least one activity from each topic area.
- You may not do more than two activities in any one topic area for credit. (You are, of course, welcome to do more than two for your own investigation.)
- Grading will be ongoing, so turn in products as you complete them.
- All free-choice proposals must be turned in and approved *prior* to working on that free choice.
- You must earn 120 points for a 100%. You may earn extra credit up to _____ points.
- You must show your plan for completion by: _____.

© Prufrock Press Inc. • *Differentiating Instruction With Menus: Math* • *Grades 3–5*
Permission is granted to photocopy or reproduce this page for single classroom use only.

Measurement

Name:_____

Length	Capacity	Weight	Time	Temperature	Points for Each Level
☐ Create a mind map that shows the different units of length and appropriate examples for each. (10 pts.)	☐ Design your own version of the Gallon Person. Give him or her a personality! (15 pts.)	☐ Create a windowpane for six classroom items. Record your estimation of their weight and their actual weight. (10 pts.)	☐ Make a mobile that shows the importance of telling time. Include practical and creative examples. (10 pts.)	☐ Create a worksheet that quizzes your classmates on their ability to read a thermometer and predict temperatures. (10 pts.)	10–15 Points
☐ Create a map of your room. (You may have to do some measuring!) Develop a scale for your map using appropriate units. (25 pts.)	☐ Collect four household items that are measured in milliliters and four measured in liters. This will give you a total of eight items to bring to class. (20 pts.)	☐ Collect and weigh 10 different items. You must have at least one that weighs one gram, one kilogram, one ounce, and one pound. (20 pts.)	☐ Using your birth date and the day and time this project was assigned, express your age in minutes and seconds. (25 pts.)	☐ Cut out the national temperature chart in your newspaper for one week. Create a graph to show how the temperature has changed in three cities throughout the week. (20 pts.)	20–25 Points
☐ Design a new unit for measuring length. Create a brochure that explains the unit, tells how it is measured, and provides equivalents to our current units. (30 pts.)	☐ Create an activity in which your classmates would practice estimating and measuring cups, pints, quarts, and gallons. (30 pts.)	☐ Bridges always have weight restrictions for safety. Investigate different bridge designs and create a bridge model that can hold more than 10 kilograms. (30 pts.)	☐ Create the perfect schedule for a week. It should be designed for people your age and all the interests they have. Note: You must go to school and you must sleep! (30 pts.)	☐ Design your own lesson on measuring temperature. It should be a lesson that can be taught at school. (30 pts.)	30 Points
Free Choice (prior approval) (25–50 pts.)	**Free Choice** (prior approval) (25–50 pts.)	**Free Choice** (prior approval) (25–50 pts.)	**Free Choice** (prior approval) (25–50 pts.)	**Free Choice** (prior approval) (25–50 pts.)	25–50 Points
Total:	Total:	Total:	Total:	Total:	Total Grade:

© Prufrock Press Inc. • *Differentiating Instruction With Menus: Math • Grades 3–5*
Permission is granted to photocopy or reproduce this page for single classroom use only.

CHAPTER 10

Problem Solving

Problem-Solving Strategies

2-5-8 Menu

Objectives Covered Through This Menu and These Activities
- Students will be able to identify different ways to solve problems.
- Students will be able to evaluate different problem-solving techniques and their effectiveness.

Materials Needed by Students for Completion
- Video camera (for commercial)
- Microsoft PowerPoint or other slideshow software
- Cube template

Time Frame
- 1–2 weeks—Students are given the menu as the unit is started, and the teacher discusses all of the product options on the menu. As the different options are discussed, students will choose products that add to a total of 10 points. As the lessons progress through the week, the teacher and the students should refer back to the options associated with the content being taught.
- 1–2 days—The teacher chooses an activity from the menu to use with the entire class.

Suggested Forms
- All-purpose rubric
- Proposal form for point-based projects

Name:_____

Problem-Solving Strategies

Directions: Choose two activities from the menu below. The activities must total 10 points. Place a check mark in each box to show which activities you will complete. All activities must be completed by _____.

2 Points

- ❒ Create a problem-solving cube. Put one strategy and an example on each side of the cube.

- ❒ Create a flipbook of problem-solving strategies. On each page, record an example of each strategy.

5 Points

- ❒ How do you know which strategy works best for which problem? Develop a brochure that explains the different problem-solving strategies and how a student could decide which strategy is best.

- ❒ Create a PowerPoint presentation that shows the most common problem-solving strategies. Include an example of a problem best solved by each strategy.

- ❒ Using a Venn diagram, compare and contrast two problem-solving strategies.

- ❒ Free choice—Prepare a proposal form and submit to your teacher for approval.

8 Points

- ❒ Although there are many problem-solving techniques, everyone has a preference. Which technique do you find the most helpful? Create a commercial for this technique. Include specific reasons why you feel that strategy is the best.

- ❒ Prepare a lesson for your classmates on the different types of problem-solving strategies and how to use each one.

Problem-Solving Cube

Complete the cube for different problem-solving strategies. Use this pattern or create your own cube. Each side of the cube should have one strategy and an example of how to use that strategy to solve problems.

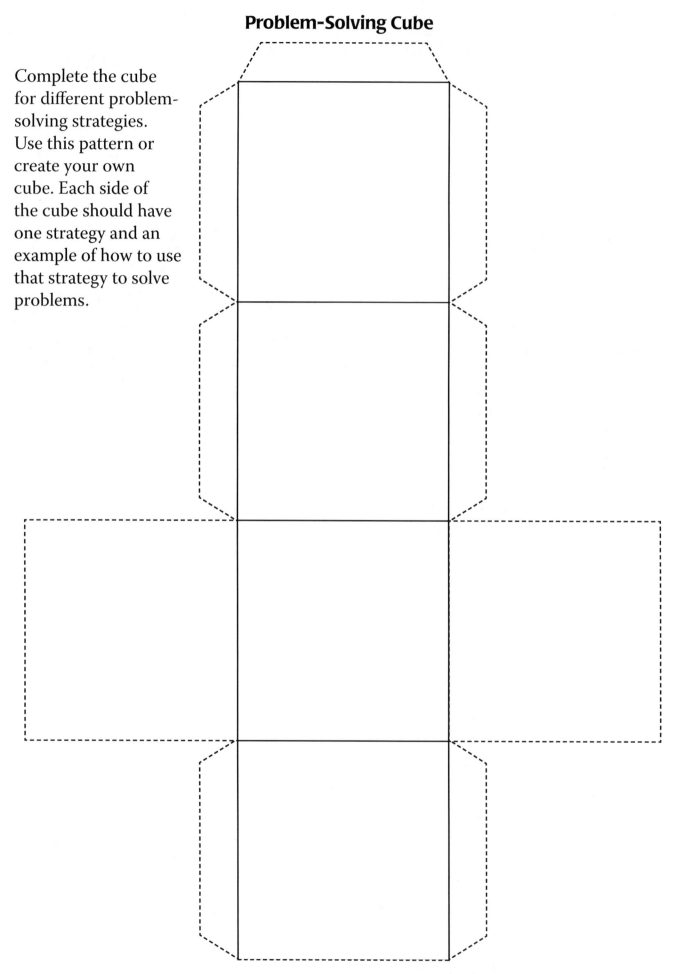

© Prufrock Press Inc. • *Differentiating Instruction With Menus: Math • Grades 3–5*
Permission is granted to photocopy or reproduce this page for single classroom use only.

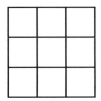

Famous Mathematicians

Tic-Tac-Toe Menu

Objective Covered Through This Menu and These Activities
- Students will be able to identify and investigate famous mathematicians and their contributions.

Materials Needed by Students for Completion
- Video camera (for news report commercial)
- Microsoft PowerPoint or other slideshow software
- Blank index cards (for trading cards)
- Scrapbooking materials
- List of famous mathematicians appropriate for grades 3–5 (see Famous Mathematicians)

Time Frame
- 2 weeks—Students are given the menu as the unit is started. As the teacher presents lessons throughout the week, students refer back to the options associated with that content. The teacher will go over all of the options for that content and have students place check marks in the boxes that represent the activities they are most interested in completing. As teaching continues throughout the 2 weeks, the activities chosen and completed should make a column or a row.
- 1 week—At the start of the unit, the teacher chooses the three activities he or she feels are most valuable for the students. Stations can be set up in the classroom. These three activities are available for student choice throughout the week, as regular instruction takes place.
- 1–2 days—The teacher chooses an activity from the menu to use with the entire class.

Suggested Forms
- All-purpose rubric
- Proposal form for projects

Famous Mathematicians

☐ *Design a Windowpane*	☐ *Create a Scrapbook*	☐ *You Be the Star!*
After folding a piece of paper into six boxes, choose six mathematicians that were important to our current unit of study. Record the mathematicians' names and three facts about them in each windowpane.	Choose one mathematician that you feel has had the largest impact on the study of mathematics. Create a scrapbook about this mathematician's life and accomplishments.	Research a famous mathematician. Prepare a You Be the Person presentation for your class.
☐ *Create a PowerPoint*	☐ **Free Choice**	☐ *Write a Newspaper Article*
Choose one significant mathematician from our current unit of study. Create a PowerPoint presentation to accompany a speech on your chosen mathematician and his or her contributions to the study of mathematics.	(Fill out your proposal form before beginning the free choice!)	You have been asked to interview a famous mathematician from our current unit of study. Develop appropriate interview questions and write a newspaper article with the information about the mathematician and his or her discoveries.
☐ *Perform a News Report*	☐ *Design a Book Cover*	☐ *Create Trading Cards*
A mathematician from our current unit of study is being nominated for the "Mathematicians Hall of Fame." Prepare a news report on the mathematician and why he or she is qualifying for this special honor.	There is a new biography being written about a well-known mathematician. Design a book cover for this mathematician's biography.	Create a set of trading cards for at least 10 mathematicians who made significant contributions to the study of mathematics.

Check the boxes you plan to complete. They should form a tic-tac-toe across or down.
All products are due by: _____.

© Prufrock Press Inc. • *Differentiating Instruction With Menus: Math • Grades 3–5*
Permission is granted to photocopy or reproduce this page for single classroom use only.

Name:_____

Famous Mathematicians

Archimedes	Charles Babbage	Benjamin Banneker
Countess of Lovelace (Augusta Ada King)	René Descartes	Persi Diaconis & Pau Erdös
Euclid	Leonhard Euler	Fibonacci
Sophie Germain	Thomas Hobbes	Herman Hollerith
Hypatia of Alexandria	John Kemeny	John Forbes Nash
Blaise Pascal	Plato	Pythagoras
Julia Robinson		

Euclid

© Prufrock Press Inc. • *Differentiating Instruction With Menus: Math* • *Grades 3–5*
Permission is granted to photocopy or reproduce this page for single classroom use only.

References
& Resources

References

Anderson, L., & Krathwohl, D. (Eds.). (2001). *A taxonomy for learning, teaching, and assessing: A revision of Bloom's taxonomy of educational objectives* (Complete ed.). New York, NY: Longman.

Keen, D. (2001). *Talent in the new millennium: Report on year one of the programme.* Retrieved from http://www.dce.ac.nz/research/content_talent.htm

Magner, L. (2000). Reaching all children through differentiated assessment: The 2-5-8 plan. *Gifted Child Today, 23*(3), 48–50.

Resources

Assouline, S., & Lupkowski-Shoplik, A. (2005). *Developing math talent: A guide for educating gifted and advanced learners in math.* Waco, TX: Prufrock Press.

Bollow, N., Berg, R., & Tyler, M. W. (2000). *Alien math.* Waco, TX: Prufrock Press.

Conway, J. H. (1996). *The book of numbers.* New York, NY: Copernicus.

Fadiman, C. (1962). *The mathematical magpie.* New York, NY: Simon and Schuster.

Field, A. (2006). *The great math experience: Engaging problems for middle school mathematics.* Victoria, BC: Trafford.

Kleiman, A., & Washington, D. (with Washington, M. F.). (1996). *It's alive and kicking . . . math the way it ought to be—tough, fun, and a little weird.* Waco, TX: Prufrock Press.

Kleiman, A., & Washington, D. (with Washington, M. F.). (1996). *It's alive! Math like you've never known it before . . . and like you may never know it again.* Waco, TX: Prufrock Press.

Lee, M. (1997*). Real-life math investigations.* New York, NY: Scholastic.

Lee, M. (2001). *40 fabulous math mysteries kids can't resist (grades 4–8).* New York, NY: Scholastic.

Miller, M., & Lee, M. (1998). *Problem solving and logic: Great skill-building activities, games, and reproducibles.* New York, NY: Scholastic.

Pappas, T. (1989). *The joy of mathematics: Discovering mathematics all around you.* San Carlos, CA: Wide World Publishing.

Pappas, T. (1993). *Fractals, googols and other mathematical tales.* San Carlos, CA: Wide World Publishing.

Pappas, T. (1997). *Mathematical scandals.* San Carlos, CA: Wide World Publishing.

Schwartz, D. M. (1998). *G is for googol: A math alphabet book.* Berkeley, CA: Tricycle Press.

Scieszka, J., & Smith, L. (1995). *Math curse.* New York, NY: Viking Books.

Washington, M. F. (1995). *Real life math mysteries.* Waco, TX: Prufrock Press.

Zaccaro, E. (2003a). *Primary grade challenge math.* Bellevue, IA: Hickory Grove Press.

Zaccaro, E. (2003b). *The ten things all future mathematicians and scientists must know (but are rarely taught).* Bellevue, IA: Hickory Grove Press.

Zaccaro, E. (2005). *Challenge math for the elementary and middle school student* (2nd ed.). Bellevue, IA: Hickory Grove Press.

Zaccaro, E. (2006). *Becoming a problem solving genius.* Bellevue, IA: Hickory Grove Press.

About the Author

After teaching science for more than 15 years, both overseas and in the U.S., **Laurie E. Westphal** now works as an independent gifted education and science consultant nationwide. She enjoys developing and presenting staff development on differentiation for various districts and conferences, working with teachers to assist them in planning and developing lessons to meet the needs of all students. Laurie currently resides in Houston, TX, and has made it her goal to convert as many teachers as she can to the differentiated lifestyle in the classroom and share her vision for real-world, product-based lessons that help all students become critical thinkers and effective problem solvers.

If you are interested in having Laurie speak at your next staff development day or conference, please visit her website, http://www.giftedconsultant.com, for additional information.

Common Core State Standards Alignment

This book aligns with an extensive number of the Common Core State Standards in Math. Please visit http://www.prufrock.com/ccss to download a complete packet of the standards that align with each individual menu in this book.

Additional Titles by the Author

Laurie E. Westphal has written many books on using differentiation strategies in the classroom, providing teachers of grades K–8 with creative, engaging, ready-to-use resources. Among them are:

Differentiating Instruction With Menus, Grades K–2
(Math, Language Arts, Science, and Social Studies volumes available)

Differentiating Instruction With Menus, Grades 3–5
(Math, Language Arts, Science, and Social Studies volumes available)

Differentiating Instruction With Menus, Grades 6–8
(Math, Language Arts, Science, and Social Studies volumes available)

Differentiating Instruction With Menus for the Inclusive Classroom, Grades K–2
(Math, Language Arts, Science, and Social Studies volumes available Spring 2013)

Differentiating Instruction With Menus for the Inclusive Classroom, Grades 3–5
(Math, Language Arts, Science, and Social Studies volumes available Spring 2012)

Differentiating Instruction With Menus for the Inclusive Classroom, Grades 6–8
(Math, Language Arts, Science, and Social Studies volumes available Fall 2012)

**For a current listing of Laurie's books, please visit
Prufrock Press at http://www.prufrock.com.**